Workbook/Laboratory Manual

FOURTH EDITION

Intercambios

Spanish for Global Communication

Michelle Evers
Creighton University

Guiomar Borrás A.
Thunderbird—The American Graduate School of International Management

James N. Hendrickson

Australia • Canada • Mexico • Singapore • Spain • United Kingdom • United States

Intercambios, **4/e**
Workbook/Laboratory Manual
Evers / Borrás A. / Hendrickson

Acquisitions Editor: Helen Richardson
Managing Editor: Glenn Wilson
Senior Production Editor: Esther Marshall
Director of Marketing: Lisa Kimball
Marketing Manager: Jill Garrett
Manufacturing Manager: Marcia Locke
Compositor: Pre-Press Company, Inc.
Project Manager: Kris Swanson
Cover Designer: Ha Nguyen
Printer: Patterson Printing

Printed in the United States of America
3 4 5 6 7 8 9 10 06 05

For more information contact Heinle, 25 Thomson Place, Boston, MA 02210 USA,
or you can visit our Internet site at http://www.heinle.com

ISBN 0-8384-2509-7

Text Credits
Lección 2: "Estudia tu vocación", *Clara, mensual con mil ideas,* No. 44, mayo 1996. **Lección 3:** "Los españoles trabajamos más horas", *Clara, mensual con mil ideas,* No. 43, abril 1996. **Lección 7:** "El submarinismo", *Clara, mensual con mil ideas,* No. 44, mayo 1996. **Lección 9:** "Ideas de navidad", *La opinión,* 7 de diciembre de 1989; "Cartitas a Santa Claus", por Arturo Olmedo, *El Excelsior del Condado de Orange,* 22 de diciembre de 1993. **Lección 14:** "Médico de familia" y "La aspirina", *Clara, mensual con mil ideas,* No. 58, julio de 1997. **Lección 15:** "Veraneantes solidarios", *Clara, mensual con mil ideas,* No. 58, julio de 1997.

Clip art from Macromedia Freehand and Image Club was used in the production of this publication.

Contents

Preface

The *Workbook/Laboratory Manual* for the fourth edition of ***Intercambios: Spanish for Global Communication*** by Guiomar Barrás Álvarez and James M. Hendrickson is designed to practice and reinforce the concepts and skills introduced in the main text. The manual provides additional practice in developing vocabulary and grammar usage, listening comprehension, and reading and writing skills. The *Actividades y ejercicios orales* sections (and accompanying audio program) are designed to improve students' oral proficiency, with emphasis on learning strategies to understand and reproduce authentic oral discourse in Spanish. Presented throughout the *Workbook/Laboratory Manual* are many notes to the student suggesting areas to recall or review, giving study hints and glossing new vocabulary words.

The *Workbook/Laboratory Manual* contains sixteen lessons *(Lección preliminar* and *Lecciones 1–15)* that correspond to the sixteen lessons presented in the main text of ***Intercambios: Spanish for Global Communication*, Fourth edition.** Each lesson in the *Workbook/Laboratory Manual* contains the following sections:

- *Vocabulario esencial* provides discrete point exercises and productive activities aimed at vocabulary practice.
- *Gramática esencial* reinforces the two or three major grammatical structures of Spanish that are introduced in each lesson in the main textbook. These exercises are designed to help students manipulate grammatical structures in written form so that they can visualize how the various structures work within a situational context.
- *Cultura* reinforces the cultural content of the main text. While culture is presented in a variety of formats in the textbook (within *En contexto* dialogs, *Notas del texto, Cultura* boxes, and *Perspectivas* sections), students have an opportunity to recall and synthesize what they've learned in the *Cultura* section of the workbook. This section combines a variety of exercise formats with an occasional cultural reading that expands upon the content covered in the chapter.
- *¡A leer!* is designed to practice reading strategies in Spanish using authentic material. Each *¡A leer!* section is divided into three subsections. The *Antes de leer* activities are designed so that students can benefit from pre-reading activities that focus on the topic of the authentic text. This section includes in-class activities and techniques that make use of students' existing knowledge of the world and allow them to brainstorm and produce ideas that might appear in the authentic text. In *Lección preliminar* and *Lecciones 1–3,* the activities are to be completed in English. Beginning in *Lección 4,* the students have acquired enough vocabulary to brainstorm in the target language. The *Vamos a leer* section requires the active participation of the students by encouraging them to use their relevant background information to read authentic texts in Spanish. The reading may be an in-class or out-of-class activity; however, it is important that students do not attempt to read word-for-word, but rather utilize the reading techniques suggested in the *¡A leer!* sections in the main textbook. In particular, the skimming and scanning strategies will help students acquire a global view of the text. The *Después de leer* activities allow students to go beyond the factual details of the text. These post-reading activities place students in contact with the material

in realistic settings by means of role play and other activities designed to integrate and personalize information gained from the authentic texts. This final stage links the development of reading skills to development of listening, speaking, and writing skills.

- *¡A escribir!* is divided into three sections. In *Antes de escribir,* students brainstorm ideas about a topic that has been introduced in the lesson from the main textbook. In *Vamos a escribir,* they write about their own experiences or about a situation in which the characters from the main textbook find themselves. In *Después de escribir,* students reflect, share, and examine what they have written. In several instances, a peer editing activity is included that is designed to be done in class.

- *Pronunciación esencial* appears in the first ten lessons *(Lección preliminar* and *Lecciones 1–9)* to provide practice in pronouncing the Spanish sounds that are the most problematic for native speakers of English. These sounds are integrated into short dialogs based on the characters and situations introduced in the main text. The dialogs provide samples of authentic discourse in Spanish and are designed to develop students' pronunciation in Spanish well enough to be understood by native speakers who have had little or no contact with non-native speakers. Native speakers of Spanish have recorded the dialogs in this section on the *Laboratory Audio Program* (available on compact disc).

- *En contexto* dialogs, similar in content to the *En contexto* dialogs in the main text, give students exposure to aural input that contextualizes new chapter content. Students work with the same story line, structures, vocabulary, and topics found in the main text, and demonstrate mastery over new material by completing questions in a variety of formats: true/false, fill-in-the-blank, multiple-choice.

Nombre ______________________________ Fecha ______________

LECCIÓN PRELIMINAR

Cuaderno de ejercicios

VOCABULARIO ESENCIAL

WP-1 Meeting and Greeting People in Your Class. Choose the best response for each situation described. Put the letter of that response in the space provided.

a. la mochila
b. Escuche a la profesora.
c. ¡Buenos días! ¿Qué tal?
d. Abran el libro en la página 18.
e. Siéntense, por favor.
f. Muéstreme la tarea, por favor.

1. _______ You have just arrived at class at 9:00 in the morning. You greet another student.
2. _______ Your professor is ready to begin the lesson. She wants you to take your seats.
3. _______ Now your professor wants you to look in your book.
4. _______ You are visiting with your neighbor during class. She asks you to stop talking and listen to your professor.
5. _______ Your professor wants to see that you have completed the homework.
6. _______ What do you use to carry your books to class?

WP-2 Los números. Write out the following numbers in Spanish.

1. 25 ______________ 2. 14 ______________ 3. Your telephone number ______________

GRAMÁTICA ESENCIAL

WP-3 Indefinite Articles: Personas famosas. Complete the following sentences with the appropriate indefinite article **(un, una).** Some Spanish nouns always end in **-a,** whether they are referring to a man or a woman. For example: **un artista / una artista.** Pay attention to the gender of the famous people in this activity.

1. Isabel Allende es ______________ autora chilena.
2. Carlos Fuentes es ______________ novelista mexicano.
3. Pedro Almodóvar es ______________ director español.
4. Maradona es ______________ futbolista argentino.
5. Pablo Neruda es ______________ poeta chileno.
6. Shakira es ______________ cantante colombiana.

Nombre ______________________ Fecha ____________

WP-4 Definite and Indefinite Articles: Personas y productos. Complete the following sentences with appropriate definite articles **(el, la, los, las)** or indefinite articles **(un, una, unos, unas).**

1. __________ líderes *(leaders)* del mundo son responsables.
2. __________ presidente de Francia es inteligente.
3. __________ presidente de Nicaragua es interesante.
4. Costa Rica es __________ país fascinante.
5. Kiwi es __________ fruta de Nueva Zelanda.
6. __________ papaya es __________ fruta tropical.
7. __________ teléfonos de Taiwán son fantásticos.
8. __________ computadoras de los Estados Unidos son excelentes.
9. __________ autos de Corea son prácticos y buenos.
10. __________ bicicletas de Italia son maravillosas.

WP-5 Cultura. Answer the following questions based on the cultural readings from your textbook.

1. Can you name the capitals of the following countries: Mexico, Spain, Argentina, Costa Rica?

   ____

2. Name three countries in the world where Spanish is the official language.

   ____

3. Mention some of the ancient languages that have influenced Spanish.

   ____

¡A leer!: Mercosur

WP-6 Skimming and Scanning. Skimming and scanning are important reading techniques used to gather information quickly. Skim the Aerolíneas Sur advertisement to get the gist or general idea of its content. Next, scan the advertisement to find the specific information asked of you in the questions below. Finish by reading carefully to fill in the rest of the information.

Antes de leer

WP-7 Can you answer these questions even before carefully reading the Aerolíneas Sur advertisement? Use the information in English in the box on the next page.

1. What does Mercosur mean?

   ____

2. What countries in Latin America belong to Mercosur?

   ____

3. What are the goals of this group?

   ____

Nombre ______________________ Fecha ______________

Mercosur

Merosur is the name for the Southern Common Market. The countries that belong to this group now are: Argentina, Paraguay, Uruguay, and Brazil. Chile, Bolivia, Venezuela, Colombia, and Peru have also shown great interest in joining. The member countries of Mercosur have a combined population of 190 million people living in an area larger than the total surface of the European continent. Some of Mercosur's goals are the free transit of goods, the elimination of customs rights, and open competition among the member countries.

DIARIO AL MERCOSUR Y

SGO. DE CHILE

Aerolíneas Sur le ofrece la mejor forma de llegar al centro de sus negocios en la capital de Chile. Con las ventajas y beneficios de la Clase Club y la comodidad de su nueva generación de asientos. Sume puntos con su tarjeta Aerolíneas Plus. Aerolíneas Sur, su línea directa con el Mercosur. Si desea más información, **consulte en suagencia de viajes** o llame a Aerolíneas Sur: Tel.: (91) 444 47 33, Internet: Http://WWW.AEROLINEAS.SUR.COM.AR.

WP-8 Find this information without spending too much time deciphering the whole advertisement.

1. What do they call the map in the ad? ______________________
2. What is the name of the airline? ______________________
3. What is the Internet address? ______________________
4. What countries does this airline visit? ______________________

Después de leer

WP-9 Now that you have read the ad in greater detail, think about what the airline is offering.

1. If you were flying with Aerolíneas Sur, to which city or cities would you like to travel and why?

   ____

2. Why do you think Aerolíneas Sur wants to fly to the countries that belong to Mercosur?

   ____

3. What type of people will go to these countries?

   ____

4. What do you think are the advantages of flying the Club Class?

   ____

¡A escribir!

Antes de escribir

WP-10 Look at the map below and list five countries you would like to visit.

1. ______________________
2. ______________________
3. ______________________
4. ______________________
5. ______________________

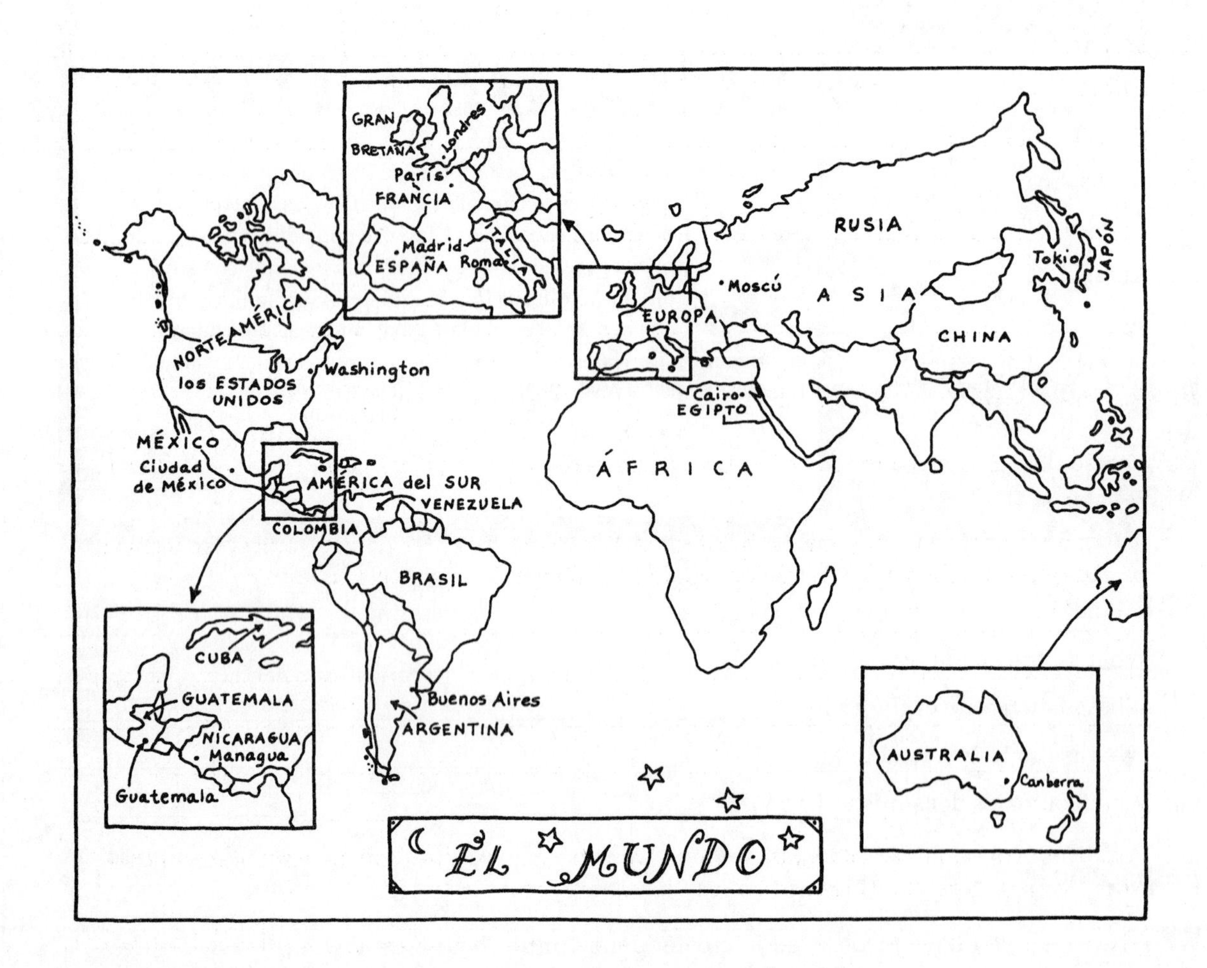

Vocabulary: continents; countries
Grammar: articles: definite; indefinite

Vamos a escribir

WP-11 Use the map to find the capital of each country listed below and write a short sentence for each one.

Ejemplo: Egipto
La capital de Egipto es el Cairo.

1. México
____

2. España
____

3. Francia
____

4. Costa Rica
____

5. Cuba
____

Después de escribir

WP-12 Use the lines provided to write your responses or you may use ***Atajo:** Writing Assistant for Spanish.*

1. Select one country from your list in Exercise WP-10 on the previous page and write a short paragraph in English about why you would like to visit that particular country.
____
____
____
____
____

2. Read the paragraph you have just written. Do you already know how to write some of the words you used above in Spanish? If so, list them here.
____
____
____

3. Share the **Antes de escribir** and **Después de escribir** exercises with a fellow student. Working together, can you come up with additional Spanish words to add to your lists from item 2 above?
____
____
____
____
____

Nombre ____________________ Fecha ____________

Actividades y ejercicios orales

PRONUNCIACIÓN ESENCIAL

CD1-2 **WP-13** The alphabet is the best place to start learning the sounds of a new language. It will be helpful to know the alphabet when you need to spell your name or your address in Spanish. It will also help you when you want to know how to spell a word in order to look up its meaning. Listed below are the letters of the Spanish alphabet along with their names. Repeat the letters after they have been modeled.

a	a	j	jota	r	ere
b	be	k	ka	s	ese
c	ce	l	ele	t	te
d	de	m	eme	u	u
e	e	n	ene	v	ve
f	efe	ñ	eñe	w	doble ve
g	ge	o	o	x	equis
h	hache	p	pe	y	i griega
i	i	q	cu	z	zeta

CD1-3 **WP-14** Pronounce these first and last names and then spell them.

Ejemplo: Robin Morán
ere, o, be, i, ene; eme, o, ere, a, ene

Joe Santiago
Alison Marks
Reed Wynne
Carmen Miranda
Carlos Fuentes
Pepe LePeu
Dolores Fridman
Cornelia Zavala
Yuspi Zavarse
Sonia Morales

WP-15 Write your first name, last name, and address. Then practice spelling them aloud.

____

____

____

EN CONTEXTO

CD1-4 **WP-16 Saludos.** You will hear a short conversation between two students. Based only on the information you hear, decide whether the statements below are true (**V: verdadero**), false (**F: falso**), or whether there is not sufficient information to decide (**N: no hay información suficiente**), and write down the corresponding letter next to each statement.

____ 1. Los estudiantes se llaman Raúl y Ben.

____ 2. Raúl es de Nuevo México.

____ 3. Antonio es de Nueva York.

____ 4. Antonio y Alex son amigos.

____ 5. Ellos son canadienses.

Nombre ______________________________ Fecha ______________

VOCABULARIO ESENCIAL

CD1-5 **WP-17 Saludar y conocer a tus compañeros(as) de clase.** You will hear three conversations. Write the number of the conversation below the picture it matches. (Look at the pictures while you listen and consider everything you see and hear.)

______

______

______

CD1-6 **WP-18 Las nacionalidades.** Listen to the following nationalities and repeat them after the speaker on the tape. Pronunciation takes practice and experience with the language. Try to match your pronunciation of these words as closely to the pronunciation of the native speaker on the CD as you can.

árabe
chino
japonesa
costarricense
guatemalteca
hondureño
nicaragüense

cubana
dominicano
puertorriqueña
argentino
boliviana
chileno
colombiano

alemana
español
francesa
griego
holandesa
inglés
estadounidense

Nombre ______________________________ Fecha ______________

CD1-7 **WP-19 Los países y las nacionalidades.** Listen to the name of each country and circle the nationality that corresponds. You will hear the name of the country twice.

Ejemplo: *You hear:* el Canadá
You circle: (canadiense)

	canadiense	estadounidense	griego
1.	boliviano	cubano	peruano
2.	uruguayo	venezolano	salvadoreño
3.	portugués	argentino	panameño
4.	indú	inglés	mexicano
5.	guatemalteco	ruso	paraguayo
6.	canadiense	mexicano	estadounidense
7.	griego	guatemalteco	colombiano
8.	costarricense	puertorriqueño	ruso
9.	salvadoreño	panameño	hondureño
10.	argentino	español	portugués

CD1-8 **WP-20 ¿Cómo te llamas?** You will hear five questions or phrases. Circle the appropriate answer to each.

Ejemplo: *You hear:* ¿Cómo te llamas?
You circle:

	Soy de Minnesota.	(Me llamo Kelly.)	Bien.
1.	Buenas tardes.	Buenas noches.	Buenos días.
2.	Adiós.	Hola.	Gracias.
3.	Bien, gracias.	Soy de Colorado.	Me llamo Sara.
4.	Más o menos, gracias.	Adiós, gracias.	Buenas tardes, gracias.
5.	Muy bien, gracias.	Soy del Canadá.	Me llamo Mary Ellen.

CD1-9 **WP-21 En la clase.** You will hear eight commands. Write the number of the command below the picture it matches. (Look at the pictures while you listen and consider everything you see and hear.)

____

____

____

____

____

____

____

____

Nombre ______________________ Fecha ____________

PASO 1 Nuevos amigos en México

LECCIÓN 1 ¡BIENVENIDA A MONTERREY!

Cuaderno de práctica

VOCABULARIO ESENCIAL

W1-1 Greetings and Good-byes. Fill in the blanks to complete the following conversation. Select from the list of expressions below.

Encantado.	Bien, gracias.	¿Cómo te llamas?
El gusto es mío.	Hasta luego.	Me llamo Javier.
Hola.		

Enrique: Hola, Alicia. Me llamo Enrique González.

Alicia: ¡____________! ¡Mucho gusto!

Enrique: ____________. ¿Qué tal?

Alicia: ____________. ¿Cómo está usted?

Enrique: Bien, gracias. Quiero presentarte a mi hijo.

Alicia: Hola. ¿____________?

Javier: ____________. Hola, Alicia. ____________.

Alicia: Mucho gusto.

Enrique y Javier: Bueno, adiós, y hasta mañana.

Alicia: ¡____________!

W1-2 Personal Titles. Provide the correct title for the following people according to the information given. Select from the list below.

señor señora señorita doctor don doña

1. Alicia Benson, estudiante, 20 años ____________
2. Javier Gómez, profesor, 41 años ____________
3. Ernesto González, padre, 55 años ____________
4. Carmen, abuela *(grandmother)*, 85 años ____________
5. Jorge, abuelo *(grandfather)*, 89 años ____________
6. Emilio Fernández, médico, 42 años ____________
7. Blanca González, madre/esposa, 53 años ____________

Nombre ______________________________ Fecha ______________

Gramática esencial

W1-3 Forms of *ser*. Fill in the following blanks with the appropriate form of the verb **ser** according to the subject. Choose your answer from the word list below.

soy   eres   es   somos   sois   son

1. Patricia y yo ______________ de México.
2. Yo ______________ de Guadalajara.
3. Patricia ______________ de Monterrey.
4. Mis padres ______________ de México, D.F.
5. Vosotros ______________ de Madrid.
6. Mis primos *(cousins)* ______________ de Veracruz.

W1-4 *Ser* with Origin and Nationality. Write sentences about the following people stating where they are from. Then choose the correct nationality for the same people. Make sure that your adjective matches in gender and number with the person described.

Modelo: Rigoberta Menchú: Guatemala
Rigoberta Menchú es de Guatemala. Es guatemalteca.

1. Mel Gibson: Australia
____
2. Sting: Inglaterra
____
3. Vicente Fox: México
____
4. Andrés Galarraga: Venezuela
____
5. Gabriela Sabatini: Argentina
____
6. Shakira: Colombia
____
7. Carlos Fuentes y Octavio Paz: México
____
8. Enrique y Julio Iglesias: España
____
9. Gabriel García Márquez y Juan Valdés: Colombia
____
10. Yo: ¿... ?
____
11. Mi mejor amigo y yo: ¿... ?
____
12. Mi familia: ¿... ?
____
13. Mi profesor(a) de español: ¿... ?
____

Nombre ______________________________ Fecha ______________

W1-5 ***Ser* and Professions.** Complete the following sentences with the correct form of **ser.**

1. Alicia ______________ estudiante.
2. Ricardo y Alicia ______________ profesores de español.
3. Cristina Aguilera y Gloria Estefan ______________ cantantes.
4. Sammy Sosa ______________ jugador de béisbol.
5. Mi papá ______________ ______________.
6. Mis amigos y yo ______________ ______________.
7. Yo ______________ ______________.

W1-6 ***Ser* and Descriptive Adjectives, Adjective Agreement.** Choose from the list of adjectives below to describe the following people in your life. Then, write sentences to describe those people. Be sure to make your adjectives agree in gender and number with the people they describe. Feel free to use other adjectives that you have learned that are not listed below.

generoso(a)	guapo(a)	viejo(a)	trabajador(a)
simpático(a)	moreno(a)	bueno(a)	cortés
interesante	rubio(a)	malo(a)	honesto(a)
débil	pelirrojo(a)	bonito(a)	encantador(a)
grande	fuerte	feo(a)	
nuevo(a)	pequeño(a)	perezoso(a)	

1. Yo ____.
2. Mi mejor amigo *(My best friend)*, ______________________________.
3. Mis hermanos *(brothers and sisters)* ______________________________.
4. Mi abuela ____.
5. Mis profesores ____.
6. Mis compañeros de clase y yo ______________________________.

Cultura

W1-7 **¿Abrazos?** Read the following situations and decide which greeting would be more appropriate in the Spanish-speaking world, a handshake or a hug **(abrazo).** Circle your answer.

1. You are introduced to your classmates at the Tecnológico de Monterrey.

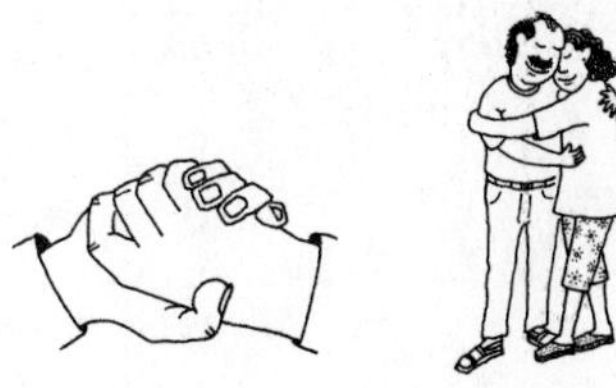

3. You visit your aunt and uncle during a family reunion.

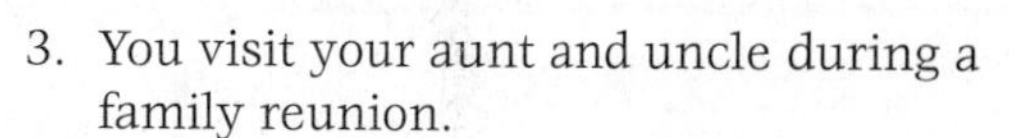

2. You run into your best friend downtown.

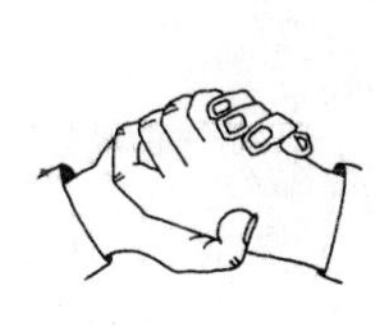

4. You greet a client at your office.

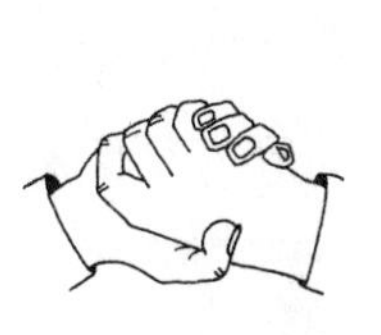

W1-8 **¿Tú o usted?** Indicate **tú** or **usted** as the appropriate form of address for the following people.

1. el profesor Gómez ______________________
2. la abuela Carmen ______________________
3. su amiga Carlota ______________________
4. el presidente Vicente Fox ______________________
5. Juan Diego, su compañero de clase ______________________

¡A leer!: Anuncios clasificados

Antes de leer

W1-9 Imagine that you are looking for a job and you want to describe yourself in a classified ad for a magazine or newspaper.

1. Make a list of the words you know in Spanish that describe you.

   ____

2. Now imagine that you've agreed to help one of your friends draft a personal ad. Make a list of the words you know in Spanish that describe your friend.

   ____

   ____

Vamos a leer

W1-10 Look at the classified ads below and on page 13 and complete the following exercise.

Sometimes when you do reading activities, it helps to read through the questions that follow before reading. That way, you know what information to focus on during your reading. Also, it may help you figure out words that you are unfamiliar with. Remember, you need not understand every word when reading. Instead, try to focus on the words that you do recognize so that you can figure out the overall meaning.

SE OFRECE

- Licenciado(a) en Ciencias Químicas.
- Diplomado(a) en Gestión Empresarial.
- Dilatada experiencia: Más de 15 años en fabricación y dirección en el sector celulosa-papel.
- Gran capacidad de trabajo. Dinámico(a) y perseverante.
  Amplia experiencia en organización y motivación de grupos humanos.
  Buenas dotes de mando y comunicación.
- Total disponibilidad y dedicación.
  No descartar otros sectores.

Apartado de Correos 11043.
50080 Zaragoza

SE OFRECE EJECUTIVO(A) PARA
DIRECTOR(A) COMERCIAL/REGIONAL/MARKETING O JEFE DE VENTAS

- ❑ Experiencia en Sector Automoción, Alimentación y Alquiler de Servicios (no descartando ningún otro sector afín).
- ❑ Idioma: Alemán.
- ❑ Disponibilidad para viajar, así como movilidad geográfica.
- ❑ Responsabilidad demostrada en multinacionales.
- ❑ Con iniciativa, dinámico(a), con experiencia en negociación grandes cuentas y en dirección, motivación y organización de equipos comerciales.

Interesados contactar al teléfono: (91) 351 31 18.

Nombre ________________________ Fecha ____________

SE OFRECE

EJECUTIVO(A)

- Licenciado(a) en derecho, diplomado(a) en CC.EE. (ICADE), MBA.
- Idioma: Inglés.
- Experiencia sector de promoción inmobiliaria.
- Informática nivel usuario.
- Experiencia en departamentos: asesoría jurídica, organización interna (ISO 9002), administración y planificación, ventas y márketing como adjunto a dirección.
- Con iniciativa, dotes para negociación, dinámico, trabajo en equipo, responsable.
- No descartar otros sectores, construcción, banca, seguros, consultoría, etc.

Interesados contactar al tel. (91) 652 19 67

1. Examine the ads and write a list of words that you recognize or whose meaning you can guess.

   ____

   ____

2. Which classified ad shows a person with responsibility?

   ____

3. Which ad shows a person who speaks English?

   ____

4. Which ad shows a person with 15 years of experience?

   ____

Después de leer

W1-11 Write the adjectives that describe the following.

1. Licenciado(a) en ciencias químicas *(B.S. in chemistry)*

   ____

2. Ejecutivo *(Executive)*

   ____

3. Director comercial / Jefe de ventas *(Sales Manager)*

   ____

4. Los mejores *(best)* adjetivos para describir a un(a) ejecutivo(a) son:

   ____

   ____

Nombre ______________________________ Fecha ______________

¡A escribir!

Antes de escribir

W1-12 Alicia Benson is greeting people first in her host family, then at the university. Complete the conversations, keeping in mind the norms for formal and informal greetings.

1. *En la casa de la familia González por la mañana*

   Alicia: ¡Buenos ____________! ¿Cómo ____________ ____________, abuelita?

   Doña Carmen: ____________ ____________. ¿Y ____________, mi hija?

   Alicia: ____________, gracias.

2. *En la universidad*

   Alicia: ¡Buenas tardes, profesor Gómez! ¿____________ ____________ usted?

   Profesor Gómez: ____________ ____________, señorita Benson. ¿Cómo ____________ usted?

   Alicia: ____________ ____________, gracias, profesor.

W1-13 Alicia Benson has just introduced you to her host parents, Ernesto and Blanca González. How do you respond to the questions below in Spanish?

1. ¿Cómo te llamas?

   ____

2. ¿De dónde eres?

   ____

3. ¿Cómo estás?

   ____

Vamos a escribir

Your class will be visited by Spanish faculty and students who are visiting the International Programs Office on your campus. Your Spanish instructor met them at a welcoming reception and invited them to visit your class to converse with the students. The following persons are scheduled to attend: Pedro Morales Ramos (a student), Carlota Ramírez Chong (a student), Doctor Germán Pérez Torres (a chemistry professor), and Justina Gonzáles (the coordinator of the exchange program). Your instructor has assigned students to write to the invited guests. Write a letter of introduction to one of them and welcome him or her to your Spanish class.

W1-14 A good way to improve your writing is to organize the ideas you want to express. In the **Lección preliminar** of ***Intercambios,*** you read and acted out many conversations with your classmates. You can use the expressions from these conversations to compose your letter of introduction. First, make a list of the phrases you would use to greet others and to introduce yourself. Next, make a list of expressions you would use to say where people are from and to welcome people to your Spanish class. Finally, make a list of any other information you would like to include in your letter. You have now organized the essential ideas you need in Spanish and are ready to begin writing your letter to your invited guest.

1. Expressions you would use to greet others and introduce yourself:

____

____

____

2. Expressions to say where people are from and to welcome them:

____

____

____

3. Other information:

____

____

____

1-15 Use the information below to write your letter in the space provided.

1. Greet the guest **(Estimado[a] señor[a], doctor[a])**
2. Introduce yourself. State your name, say that you are a student and where, and say where you are from. Include additional biographical information.
3. Welcome him/her to the university and to your Spanish class **(Bienvenido[a] a...).**
4. Include a closing **(Cordialmente** or **Sinceramente).**
5. Sign your name.

____

____

____

____

____

____

____

Después de escribir

1-16 With a classmate, edit the letter you have written. Look for subject/verb agreement every time the verb **ser** is used. Also watch for adjective agreement with gender and number.

Nombre ______________________________ Fecha ______________

Actividades y ejercicios orales

PRONUNCIACIÓN ESENCIAL

CD1-10 **Spanish *a, o, u***

Spanish vowels are always short, crisp, and tense. They do not have glide sounds as in the English word *go*.

W1-17 Spanish **a** is pronounced approximately like the *a* in *father*. Listen to the following sentences and repeat after the speaker.

—¡Hol**a**, **A**licia!
—Buen**as** t**a**rdes, profesor**a** **A**bell**as**.
—¿Cómo est**á** tu **a**buel**a**?
—Ell**a** est**á** muy bien, gr**a**ci**as**.
—Y tu p**apá**, ¿cómo est**á**?
—Bien. ¡**A**y! ¡Tengo un**a** cl**a**se!
—H**a**st**a** m**a**ñ**a**n**a**, **A**lici**a**.
—H**a**st**a** m**a**ñ**a**n**a**, profesor**a**.

CD1-11 **W1-18** Spanish **o** is pronounced approximately like the *o* in *hope*. Listen to the following sentences and repeat after the speaker.

—¡H**o**la! Me llam**o** Dieg**o** **O**rduñ**o**.
—Mi n**o**mbre es Alicia Bens**o**n.
—Much**o** gust**o**, Alicia.
—El gust**o** es mí**o**, Dieg**o**.
—¿Cuánt**o**s añ**o**s tienes?
—Veintid**ó**s. ¿Y tú, Dieg**o**?
—Veinti**o**ch**o**. Cha**o**, Alicia.
—Cha**o**. Much**o** gust**o**.

CD1-12 **W1-19** Spanish **u** is pronounced approximately like the *u* in *tube*. Listen to the following sentences and repeat after the speaker.

—B**u**enos días, profesor Gómez.
—Hola, H**u**mberto.
—¿Cómo está **u**sted?
—M**u**y bien, H**u**mberto. Gracias.
—Quiero presentarle a mi novia, **Ú**rs**u**la.
—M**u**cho g**u**sto, **Ú**rs**u**la.
—Encantada, profesor.

Nombre ______________________ Fecha ______________

EN CONTEXTO

CD1-13 **W1-20 Bienvenida a México.** Listen to the following conversation. Based only on the information you hear, decide whether the statements below are true **(V: verdadero)**, false **(F: falso)**, or whether there is not sufficient information **(N: No hay información suficiente)**. Make sure you write down the corresponding letter next to each statement.

____ 1. La familia González es la nueva familia de Alicia.

____ 2. Doña Carmen es la mamá de Alicia.

____ 3. Ernesto es el esposo de Blanca.

____ 4. Gerardo tiene 28 años.

____ 5. Teresa estudia en el TEC.

VOCABULARIO ESENCIAL

CD1-14 **W1-21 Buenos días.** You will hear three conversations. Write the number of the conversation below the picture it matches. Look at the pictures before you begin and while you listen, considering everything you see and hear.

______ ______ ______

CD1-15 **W1-22 Los amigos de Alicia.** You will hear Alicia describe several of her classmates at the TEC. In the space provided, write the letter that corresponds to the country of origin of each student.

(Before playing the audiotape for any listening activity, scan the written portion so you will know beforehand what information to listen for.)

1. _____ Gerardo	a. México
2. _____ Adriana	b. Venezuela
3. _____ Mercedes	c. Colombia
4. _____ Arturo	d. Panamá
5. _____ Enrique	e. los Estados Unidos

CD1-16 **W1-23 ¡Mucho gusto!** Alicia has met several people in Monterrey: Blanca, Graciela, and Juan. Listen as the three of them talk about themselves, and fill in the charts below with information about each person. You will hear each description twice.

(Listen to these descriptions carefully. It is not necessary to understand every word in order to comprehend the main ideas of these descriptions. Listen for the gist of the descriptions based on the words you recognize.)

1. **Blanca**	2. **Graciela**	3. **Juan**
Edad: ______________	Origen: ______________	Origen: ______________
Ocupación: ______________	Profesión: ______________	Ocupación: ______________
¿Cómo se llama el hijo? ______________	¿Cómo se llama el esposo? ______________	Descripción de Juan: ______________ ______________ ______________
Descripción de Blanca: ______________	Descripción del esposo: ______________	

Nombre ______________________________ Fecha ______________

LECCIÓN 2 ¿TE GUSTA ESTUDIAR Y TRABAJAR EN LA UNIVERSIDAD?

Cuaderno de ejercicios

VOCABULARIO ESENCIAL

W2-1 Describe Your Friends and Classmates. Using the words from the list provided, describe the people below.

aburrido(a)	honesto(a)	trabajador(a)
ambicioso(a)	deshonesto(a)	perezoso(a)
simpático(a)	estudioso(a)	liberal
antipático(a)	extrovertido(a)	cortés
conservador(a)	tímido(a)	descortés

1. El (La) amigo(a) ideal es ______________. No es______________.
2. El (La) compañero(a) de clase perfecto es ______________. No es ______________.
3. Mi *(My)* profesor(a) favorito(a) es ______________. No es ______________.

W2-2 Academic subjects. Match each textbook with the class in which you would use it.

1. _____ *La vida de Frank Lloyd Wright*
2. _____ *Freud y tú*
3. _____ *El marxismo y el comunismo: La política y la vida*
4. _____ *Don Quixote de la Mancha*
5. _____ *Micro y macrobiología*

a. la clase de psicología
b. las clase de ciencias políticas
c. la clase de ciencia
d. la clase de arquitectura
e. la clase de literatura

GRAMÁTICA ESENCIAL

W2-3 ¿Qué tienen? Look at the drawings on page 20 and write sentences in Spanish describing what these people have. Use the correct form of the verb **tener.**

(Remember to match the form of the verb **tener** to the subject of the sentence [e.g., yo tengo].)

Ejemplo: Alicia / tener
Alicia tiene una computadora portátil.

Nombre ______________________________ Fecha ______________

1. Arturo Ayala / tener

____

____

2. Ernesto y Blanca González / tener

____

____

3. Enrique / tener

____

____

4. Trinidad y yo (nosotros[as]) / tener

____

____

5. el profesor Gómez / tener

____

____

6. tú y Gerardo (ustedes) / tener

____

____

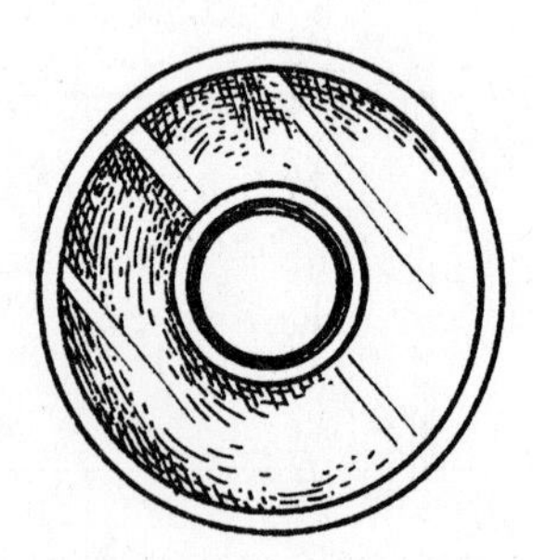

7. Alicia / tener

____

____

8. Teresa / tener

____

____

Nombre ______________________ Fecha ____________

W2-4 ¿De quién es? Use the sentences from the last exercise to answer the following questions.

1. ¿De quién es el televisor a colores?

____

2. ¿De quién es la bicicleta?

____

3. ¿De quién es el disco compacto?

____

4. ¿De quién es la computadora portátil?

____

W2-5 Personas ocupadas. Describe what these people do during the week.

Ejemplo: yo / hablar por teléfono
Yo hablo por teléfono.

1. yo / descansar por una hora

____

2. Ernesto / trabajar en la oficina

____

3. nosotros / tomar muchos exámenes

____

4. tú / escuchar a la profesora

____

5. Teresa y sus amigas / bailar en las fiestas

____

W2-6 En mi opinión. Write original sentences expressing your opinion about the following people and things. Use one word from each of the lists below and add or change the words when necessary.

Ejemplo: *Nuestras bicicletas son buenas.*

mi	televisores	es (no es)	bueno(a)
su	radio	son (no son)	moderno(a)
nuestro	profesora de español		fácil
tu	computadora		difícil
			simpático(a)
			pequeño(a)
			grande

1. ______________________
2. ______________________
3. ______________________
4. ______________________

W2-7 Me gusta / No me gusta. Adriana y Trinidad need a roommate to help out with the rent. They discuss the ideal roommate. Fill in the blanks with the correct form of the words from the list below.

Think carefully about the words you choose to fill in the blanks in this exercise. Some words will be used more than once. Some will not be used at all.

mi	me gusta	necesitar
tu	querer	hablar
su	le gusta	tener

Adriana: En ______________ opinión, nosotras ______________ una compañera de cuarto inteligente y estudiosa.

Trinidad: Nuestra amiga Raquel es inteligente, ______________ una computadora y ______________ estudiar mucho.

Adriana: Y la computadora que Raquel ______________ es de buena calidad.

Trinidad: A mí ______________ trabajar con la computadora.

Adriana: ¿ ______________ usar ______________ computadora? ¿La computadora de Raquel?

Trinidad: ¡Sí! En mi opinión, la compañera de cuarto pefecta para nosotras es Raquel... ¡porque tiene una computadora muy buena!

W2-8 Cultura. Answer the following questions in English.

1. Consider the information you read in **Lección 2** about the differences and similarities between studies in U.S. universities and those in Latin American and Spainish universities. What are two similarities?

____

____

____

2. What are two differences?

____

____

____

¡A leer!: ¡Estudia tu vocación!

Antes de leer

W2-9 Answer these questions before reading.

1. Do you know what type of profession you would like to enter? Have you discovered your vocation?

____

____

Nombre ______________________ Fecha ____________

2. Do you know what values, abilities and skills, and personality traits you need to have in order to enter the profession you have chosen?

   Values: ______________________

   ____

   Abilities and skills: ______________________

   ____

   Personality traits: ______________________

   ____

Vamos a leer

Remember, before reading it is sometimes helpful to go over the questions you will have to answer later. That way, you can focus your attention on the information you need to find.

In Spain, *informática* = *computación*

Profesiones	Asignaturas que domina	Valores	Habilidades	Personalidad
Ciencias de la salud	Matemáticas Ciencias Química	Altruismo Prestigio Buen sueldo	Científica Manual	Científica Social
Comercial Económicas	Administr. Matemáticas Informática Idiomas	Prestigio Relación Buen sueldo Responsabilidad	Liderazgo Persuasión Administrativa	Negocios
Ciencias	Matemáticas Ciencias Informática	Independencia Prestigio Variedad Creatividad	Científica Matemática Espacial	Científica
Servicios Sociales	C.Sociales Administr.	Altruismo Relación Variedad Seguridad	Persuasión Administr. Didáctica	Social
Cultura Educación	Lenguaje C.Sociales Arte Ciencias	Altruismo Creatividad Seguridad Responsabilidad	Didáctica Lingüística Social	Social
Artística	Arte Música Plástica Imagen	Creatividad Independencia Variedad Prestigio	Artística Manual Musical Lingüística	Artística
Deporte	Ed.Física Ciencias Tecnología Tiempo libre	Relación Altruismo Variedad Didáctica	Física Manual Espacial	Realista
Oficina	Contabilidad Informática Lenguaje Idiomas	Trabajo guiado Rutinas Seguridad Relación	Administr. Lingüística Concentración	Oficina

Nombre ______________________ Fecha ______________

W2-10 Answer the questions according to the information from the chart.

1. ¿En qué profesión necesitas estudiar informática o computación?
____
2. ¿Qué habilidades necesitas para las profesiones comerciales y económicas?
____
3. ¿En qué profesiones necesitas tener una personalidad realista?
____
4. ¿Qué valores necesitas tener para las profesiones científicas?
____

Después de leer

W2-11 Now, create lists of your favorite classes, your values, your abilities, and your personality traits. These lists should be helpful in guiding you toward a career choice; or, if you have already made a choice, they should help you to confirm that choice.

1. mis cursos favoritos
____
2. mis valores
____
3. mis habilidades
____
4. mi personalidad
____

¡A escribir!

Antes de escribir

W2-12 Ask a classmate the questions below and write his/her answers in Spanish.

1. ¿Cómo te llamas?	
2. ¿De dónde eres?	
3. ¿Cuántos años tienes?	
4. ¿Cómo eres?	
5. ¿Qué te gusta estudiar?	
6. ¿Cuál es tu clase favorita?	
7. ¿Cómo se llama tu compañero(a) de cuarto?	
8. ¿Tienes perros o gatos?	
9. ¿Cómo se llaman?	

Nombre ______________________________ Fecha ______________

Phrases: describing people

Vocabulary: family members; nationality; people; studies

Grammar: adjective agreement; adjective position; possesion with ***de;*** possesive adjectives; verbs: ***ser, tener,*** present tense

Vamos a escribir

W2-13 Write a paragraph about your classmate using the information that you just gathered.

Ejemplo: *Mi compañero de clase se llama Miguel. Tiene 29 años. Es trabajador y sincero. Le gusta estudiar español, pero su clase preferida es la dase de historia. Su profesora preferida se llama Michelle Evers. No tiene compañero de cuarto. Tiene dos gatos. Sus gatos se llaman el Gordo y el Flaco.*

____

____

____

____

____

____

Después de escribir

W2-14 Trade your paragraph with that of a different classmate from the one you just wrote about. Look over each other's paragraphs for the following.

1. Agreement of adjectives: Do all of the adjectives that he/she used match the noun described in gender and number?
2. Subject/verb agreement: Do all verb endings correspond to the subject(s) of each sentence?

(Note: The present tense endings for **-ar** verbs are listed on page 55 in the ***Intercambios*** textbook.)

Nombre ______________________ Fecha ______________

Actividades y ejercicios orales

Pronunciación esencial

CD1-17 ### Spanish *e, i, y*

Remember that Spanish vowels are always short, crisp, and tense.

W2-15 Spanish **e** has two pronunciations. When stressed, it is pronounced approximately like the *e* in *eight*. When unstressed, it is pronounced approximately like the *e* in *bet*. Listen to the following sentences and repeat after the speaker.

—¿Cómo s**e** llama tu compañ**e**ra?
—L**e**onor. **E**s **e**studiant**e** aquí.
—¿D**e** dónd**e** **e**s?
—**E**s d**e** Mérida, M**é**xico.
—¿Qu**é** **e**studias **e**n la univ**e**rsidad?
—Estudio **e**spañol, d**e**r**e**cho **e** ingl**é**s.

CD1-18 **W2-16** Spanish **i** and the word **y** are pronounced approximately like the *i* in *machine*. Listen to the following sentences and repeat after the speaker.

—¿Qué estud**i**as aqu**í**, Mar**í**a?
—Estud**i**o **i**nglés **y** f**i**losofía.
—**Y** yo estud**i**o med**i**c**i**na.
—¡Uy! Qué **i**nteresante, am**i**ga!
—Hay muchos estud**i**antes, ¿eh?
—S**í**. ¡En med**i**c**i**na hay muchos!

CD1-19 **W2-17** Spanish has open and closed vowels; these terms refer to how much the mouth is opened or closed when pronouncing them. When an open vowel **(a, e, o)** and a closed vowel **(i, y, u)** come together, they are pronounced as one syllable, called a diphthong (e.g., **buenos**). When an open vowel comes between two closed vowels, they are pronounced as one syllable, called a triphthong (e.g., **Uruguay**). Listen to the following sentences and repeat after the speaker.

—¡**Bue**nas noches! ¿Eres estud**ia**nte aquí en la esc**ue**la?
—Sí. Estud**io** histor**ia** y c**ie**nc**ia**s políticas. ¿Y tú?
—S**oy** estud**ia**nte tamb**ié**n. Estud**io** b**io**logía y leng**ua**s.
—¡Qué b**ue**no! S**oy** de Asunc**ió**n, Parag**uay.** ¿De dónde eres?
—S**oy** de Montevideo, Urug**uay.** Es una c**iu**dad enorme. Y tú, ¿de dónde eres?
—S**oy** de B**ue**nos **Ai**res. Es una c**iu**dad enorme tamb**ié**n.
—Sí, ¡y m**uy** bonita!

En contexto

CD1-20 **W2-18** **¿Le gusta estudiar y trabajar en México?** Listen to the following conversation. Based only on the information you hear, decide whether the statements below are true **(V: verdadero)**, false **(F: falso)**, or whether there is not sufficient information **(N: No hay información suficiente)**. Make sure you write down the corresponding letter next to each statement.

____ 1. A Alicia le gusta la clase de contabilidad.

____ 2. A Enrique le gusta la clase de contabilidad.

____ 3. El profesor de contabilidad habla rápido.

____ 4. Enrique tiene dos clases.

____ 5. Alicia enseña una clase.

Vocabulario esencial

CD1-21 **W2-19** **Los compañeros de Alicia.** Listen to the following descriptions of three of Alicia's classmates. Fill in the blanks below with the appropriate information for each one.

	¿Cuál es su nombre?	¿Cuántos años tiene?	¿De dónde es?
1.	____________	____________	____________
2.	____________	____________	____________
3.	____________	____________	____________

CD1-22 **W2-20** **Recados telefónicos.** Alicia and the González family are out of town for the weekend. Listen to the messages that their friends leave on their answering machine and write the messages in the spaces below.

1. Recado para: ______________________

   De parte de: ______________________

   Recado: ______________________

____

____

____

____

____

____

____

Nombre ______________________ Fecha ____________

2. Recado para: ______________________

   De parte de: ______________________

   Recado: ______________________

3. Recado para: ______________________

   De parte de: ______________________

   Recado: ______________________

LECCIÓN 3 ¡NECESITO UNA PASANTÍA DE TRABAJO PARA JUNIO!

Cuaderno de ejercicios

VOCABULARIO ESENCIAL

W3-1 **¿Qué hora es?** Look at the clocks below. Write out what time it is, and what activity Teresa has at that time.

Ejemplo: A las *nueve,* Teresa tiene clase de matemáticas.

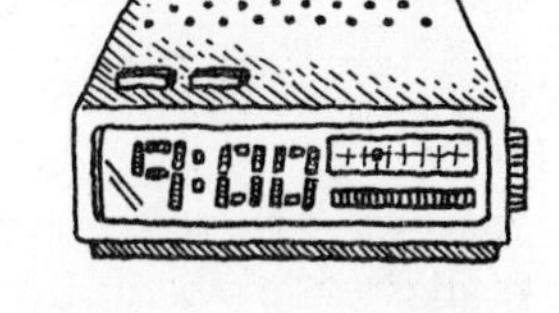

1. A las ______________________,
Teresa habla con su amiga Alicia.

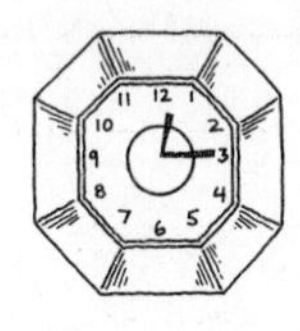

2. A las ______________________,
Teresa estudia con Enrique.

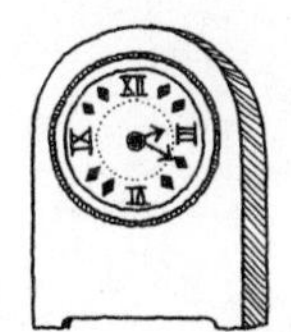

3. A las ______________________,
Teresa toma un café con su mamá.

4. A las ______________________,
Teresa tiene clase de inglés.

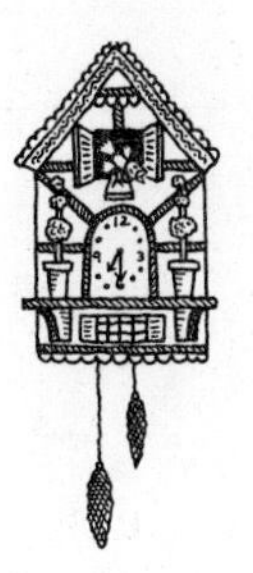

5. A las ______________________,
Teresa camina a casa.

Nombre ____ Fecha ________________

W3-2 Los días y los meses. Answer the following questions in Spanish about what days and months the following events take place.

Ejemplo: ¿Qué día de la semana es hoy *(today)*?
Hoy es martes.

1. ¿Qué días de la semana tienes clase de español?

____

2. ¿Qué días de la semana trabajas?

____

3. ¿En qué mes es tu cumpleaños *(birthday)*?

____

4. ¿En qué mes es el día de San Patricio?

____

5. ¿En qué mes es el día de San Valentín?

____

6. ¿Cuál es la fecha de hoy?

____

GRAMÁTICA ESENCIAL

W3-3 ¡Horarios llenos! Describe the activities of the following people.

Ejemplo: tú / escribir una carta
Tú escribes una carta a las nueve y quince.

1. Adriana y Arturo / comer en casa

____
____

2. yo / beber un refresco

____
____

3. nosotros / leer el periódico

____
____

4. Gerardo / deber estudiar

____
____

Nombre ______________________ Fecha ______________

W3-4 **¿Qué quieren hacer?** Alicia and her friends want to do a lot today. Write original sentences about what they want to do, following the model.

Ejemplo: Teresa / mirar la televisión
Teresa quiere mirar la televisión.

1. Alicia / correr por el parque
____
2. Blanca y Ernesto / decidir los planes para el fin de semana
____
3. Arturo / bailar salsa con su profesora
____
4. Adriana / ir al cine
____
5. Trinidad / leer el periódico
____
6. yo / estudiar para la clase de español
____

W3-5 **¿Qué van a hacer?** Look at Alicia, Arturo, and Blanca's schedule below. Fill in the column for **yo** according to what you are going to do on the days listed. Then, on page 32 write 10 original sentences stating what you, Alicia, Arturo, and Blanca plan on doing using **ir** + **a** + infinitive.

	Alicia Benson	**Arturo y Adriana**	**yo**
lunes	*enseñar inglés en el Departamento de Economía*	*mirar televisión*	
martes	*estudiar español*	*ir a la biblioteca*	
miércoles		*comer en un restaurante*	
jueves	*tomar un examen*		
viernes		*bailar en una discoteca*	
sábado	*leer el periódico*	*ir al cine*	
domingo	*descansar mucho*		

Ejemplo: *El lunes Alicia va a enseñar inglés en el Departamento de Economía.*

1. ____________________
2. ____________________
3. ____________________
4. ____________________
5. ____________________
6. ____________________
7. ____________________
8. ____________________
9. ____________________
10. ____________________

W3-6 ¡Hacemos una fiesta! Complete the following paragraph with the correct form of the verbs below. You can use these words more than once!

beber	deber	querer
comer	ir	ser

La fiesta de Arturo y Adriana

Este sábado nosotros ______________ a hacer una fiesta de cumpleaños para Arturo. Su cumpleaños ______________ el 20 de septiembre. Nosotros ______________ invitar a Alicia, a Trinidad, a Enrique y ______________ a invitar a la familia González también. La fiesta ______________ a ser a las nueve y nosotros vamos a ______________ mucha comida mexicana. También vamos a ______________ margaritas y refrescos. ¿______________ venir, Enrique?

Cultura

W3-7 Pareado. Write the letter of the correct response in the space for each of the following.

1. _____ A train that is scheduled to depart at 8:30 p.m.
2. _____ The time to arrive at a party that starts at 10:00.
3. _____ 3.12.02
4. _____ You want to know if something is starting at the exact hour given.
5. _____ A TV program listed to begin at 10:30 p.m.

a. ¿En punto?
b. el 3 de diciembre del año 2002
c. 22:30
d. 20:30
e. 22:00

Nombre ______________________________ Fecha ______________

W3-8 Los gestos. Write the correct phrase below each of the following gestures.

tacaño	¡No!
Un momento.	¡Fantástico!
Vamos a tomar.	¡Estás loco!
¡Cuidado!	dinero

1. ______________________________

2. ______________________________

3. ______________________________

4. ______________________________

5. ______________________________

6. ______________________________

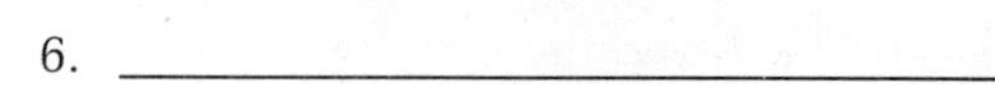

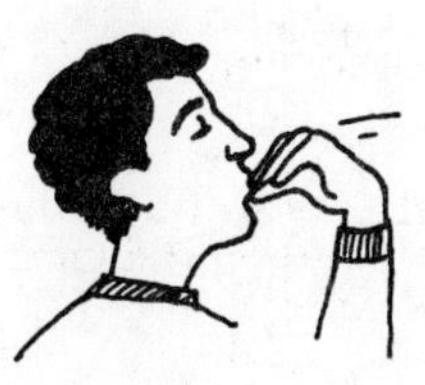

7. ______________________________

8. ______________________________

Nombre ______________________ Fecha ______________

¡A leer!: Programas de televisión

W3-9 Look at the following TV schedule from the Spanish magazine *Hola* and use the information to fill out the chart below. Remember your skimming and scanning skills from earlier chapters. First, take a look at the questions so that you know what information you are seeking.

canal sur
Televisión

08.00 TELETRASTO.
09.00 LA ISLA DE FLORA.
09.25 NOTICIAS.
09.30 LAS MAÑANAS DE CANAL SUR.
10.30 FIESTAS DE ANDALUCIA.
11.00 NOCTURNO.
12.05 ARRIBA Y ABAJO.
13.00 LAS COSAS DEL COMER.
13.10 CANCIONERO.
13.35 VECINOS
14.30 EL DIARIO-1.
15.00 EL TIEMPO.
15.05 BOLA DE DRAGON.
15.30 CINE DE TARDE: «Si fulano fuese mengano».
17.20 EL HOMBRE Y LA TIERRA.
17.40 BAHIA PELIGROSA.
18.10 BOLA DE DRAGON Z.
18.35 MIS DOS PADRES.
19.05 TAL COMO SOMOS.
20.30 EL DIARIO-2.
21.00 GRANDES EXITOS DEL CINE HISTORICO: «Alfredo El Grande».
23.35 TEMAS 7.
00.45 INDICIOS.
02.10 DESPEDIDA Y CIERRE.

TELEMADRID

07.30 TRAFICO DE MADRID.
08.50 A SABER.
10.00 TELENOTICIAS.
10.40 LA NOCHE SE MUEVE.
11.40 BELLEZA Y PODER.
12.45 LA BANDA DE LA FAMILIA BIONICA.
14.00 TELENOTICIAS MADRID.
14.30 TELENOTICIAS.
15.00 MIRA QUIEN HABLA..
15.30 CINE: «Sudie y Simpson» y «Sol negro».
19.00 AVANCE INFORMATIVO.
19.10 A TRAVES DEL ESPEJO.
20.30 TELENOTICIAS.
21.00 EN ACCION.
21.30 RAVEN, GUERRERO AMERICANO.
22.30 CINE. LA NOCHE DE PELICULA: «El gran enredo».
00.10 LA NOCHE SE MUEVE.
01.30 CINE. SALA DE MADRUGADA: «Un chico con gancho».
03.00 INFORMACION CULTURAL DE LA C. A. M.

1. ¿A qué hora es el programa *La isla de flora?* ______________ ¿En qué canal? ______________
2. ¿A qué hora hay programas de noticias? ______________ ¿En qué canal? ______________ ¿Cómo se llaman? ______________
3. ¿Qué canal tiene información cultural? ______________ ¿Cómo se llama el programa? ______________ ¿A qué hora es? ______________
4. A las 6:35 de la tarde, ¿qué hay en el Canal Sur? ______________
5. ¿Qué película hay a las 3:30 de la tarde? ______________

¡A escribir!

Antes de escribir

W3-10 Read the news item on the next page entitled "Los españoles trabajamos más horas" and answer the questions that follow.

Los españoles trabajamos más horas

Según la Oficina Estadística de las Comunidades Europeas, Eurostat, los españoles trabajamos una media de 39,2 horas a la semana. Esto significa siete horas más de trabajo que un holandés, seis horas más que un alemán y cuatro horas más que un belga. Sólo los portugueses, con 40,5 horas semanales, y los griegos con 40,1, nos superan en trabajo. Pero, curiosamente, en proporción somos los que más fiestas hacemos al año, en concreto, catorce, sólo superados por los quince días al año de los italianos.

1. ¿Qué quiere decir el título de la noticia "Los españoles trabajamos más horas"?
   ____
2. ¿Cuántas horas trabajan los españoles a la semana?
   ____
3. ¿Cuántas horas trabajan los alemanes y los holandeses?
   ____
4. ¿Cuántas horas trabajan los portugueses?
   ____
5. ¿Cuántas fiestas hacen los españoles al año? ¿Y los italianos?
   ____

Phrases: describing people
Vocabulary: nationality; personality; studies
Grammar: adjective agreement; verbs: present tense, **ser**

Vamos a escribir

W3-11 Imagine that you are asked to write a short article for your university newspaper describing the number of hours that students study per week at your institution. You will want to mention as well that many students, apart from the work that they do for their classes, also hold jobs outside of the university. Compare the hours that you and your fellow students work with the amount of work that students have at other universities you know. Write your article on a separate sheet of paper.

Los estudiantes de la Universidad X trabajamos mucho

Después de escribir

W3-12 Exchange your article with that of a classmate and correct each other's mistakes.

Nombre ______________________ Fecha ____________

Actividades y ejercicios orales

PRONUNCIACIÓN ESENCIAL

Word stress

A syllable is a word or part of a word pronounced with a single, uninterrupted sounding of the voice; for example, the word **el** has one syllable,and the word **padre** has two syllables: **pa - dre**. Word stress refers to the syllable that is most strongly stressed by the voice in a word; for example, in the word **padre,** the syllable **pa** is stressed. Spanish has three simple rules for word stress.

CD1-23 **W3-13** Words of more than one syllable ending in a vowel, **n,** or **s** are stressed on the next-to-the-last syllable. Listen to the following sentences and repeat after the speaker.

—¿**Bue**no?
—**Ho**la, Enr**i**que. **Ha**bla Ar**tu**ro. ¿**Có**mo estás?
—**Ho**la, Ar**tu**ro. ¿Qué hay de **nue**vo?
—El sábado voy a hacer **una** **fies**ta **pa**ra celebrar mi cumple**a**ños. ¿**Quie**res venir?
—Sí, **mu**chas **gra**cias. ¿A qué **ho**ra **de**bo llegar?
—Pues, **es**te... a las **nue**ve.
—Muy bien. ¡**Has**ta el sábado!
—¡**Has**ta el sábado! Chao.

CD1-24 **W3-14** Words ending in a consonant other than **n** or **s** are stressed on the last syllable. Listen to the following sentences and repeat after the speaker.

—Arturo, ¿qué vamos a ha**cer** en la fiesta?
—Este... ¡Vamos a co**mer** mucho! ¡Voy a reci**bir** muchos regalos!
—Ay, Arturo. ¿No vamos a escu**char** música? ¿No vamos a bai**lar**?
—Sí, Trini**dad**, sí. Es una fiesta, ¿no?

CD1-25 **W3-15** When a word has a stress pattern that does not follow the rules in Exercises 3-13 and 3-14, it carries a written accent mark over the stressed vowel. Question words always carry a written accent. Some one-syllable words, such as **tú** and **él,** carry an accent mark to distinguish their grammatical category and their meaning. Listen to the following sentences and repeat after the speaker.

—**Dí**game. ¿**Quién** habla?
—Hola, Adriana. Habla Alicia. ¿**Cómo** es**tás**?
—Bien, gracias. ¿Vas a ir el **sá**bado a la fiesta?
—Sí. Yo voy a ir con Gerardo. Oye, ¿**qué** necesita Arturo para su fiesta?
—Pues, no necesita más comida... ¡lo **ú**nico que necesita son sus amigos!

EN CONTEXTO

CD1-26 **W3-16 ¡Qué padre!** Listen to the following conversation. Based only on the information you hear, decide whether the statements below are true **(V: verdadero)**, false **(F: falso)**, or whether there is not sufficient information **(N: No hay información suficiente).** Make sure you write down the corresponding letter next to each statement.

1. ________ Alicia tiene planes para el sábado.
2. ________ Gerardo no tiene planes para el sábado.
3. ________ El escritor Carlos Fuentes es mexicano.
4. ________ La conferencia es en la universidad.
5. ________ La conferencia es a las 9:00 de la noche.

VOCABULARIO ESENCIAL

CD1-27 **W3-17 La vida activa de doña Carmen.** Doña Carmen is a very active woman. She keeps track of her appointments on the calendar below. Listen to her speak with her family, and write her activities on the calendar.

lunes	martes	miércoles	jueves	viernes	sábado	domingo
1	2	3	4	5	6	7
8	9	10	11	12	13	14
15	16	17	18	19	20	21
22	23	24	25	26	27	28
29	30	31				

Nombre ______________________ Fecha ______________

CD1-28 **W3-18 La fiesta de Arturo.** Arturo is going to have a party in his house to celebrate his birthday. Listen to Arturo talking about the party and write the different activities mentioned.

____________	____________	____________
____________	____________	____________
____________	____________	____________
____________	____________	____________
____________	____________	____________
____________	____________	____________

Nombre ________________________ Fecha ____________

PASO 2 Ecoturismo en Centroamérica

LECCIÓN 4 ¡TENEMOS QUE ESTAR DE ACUERDO!

Cuaderno de ejercicios

VOCABULARIO ESENCIAL

W4-1 ¡Adivina quién! *(Guess who!)* ¿Quién es la persona de la familia? Escriba el parentesco *(relationship)* de cada una de las personas siguientes.

Ejemplo: El esposo de mi abuela es mi ____*abuelo*____.

1. El hijo de mi hermano es mi ________________.
2. La hermana de mi hermano es mi ________________.
3. El esposo de mi hermana es mi ________________.
4. El hermano de mi papá es mi ________________.
5. La hermana de mi mamá es mi ________________.
6. Los padres de mis padres son mis ________________.
7. Los hijos de mis tíos son mis ________________.
8. Los hijos de mis abuelos son mis ________________.

W4-2 ¿Cuál no conuerda *(does not match)*? *(One of these things is not like the others . . .)* Mire las listas y subraye el objeto que no corresponda al grupo.

Ejemplo: la estufa, el fregadero, la cama

1. el horno, la bañera, la estufa
2. la bañera, la ducha, la mesa de noche
3. el inodoro, la cama, la mesa de noche
4. el sillón, el lavamanos, el sofá
5. la lámpara, el refrigerador, el armario

Nombre ______________________________ Fecha ______________

GRAMÁTICA ESENCIAL

W4-3 ¿Cómo y dónde están? Complete el siguiente párrafo con la forma apropiada de *estar*.

Mi amigo Tomás no ______________ casado ahora, pero quiere casarse en el futuro. Ahora, él y su novia ______________ muy contentos con su relación. Ahora, Ileana, Tomás y yo ______________ en Guatemala. Mañana vamos a ______________ en Tikal, donde ______________ las ruinas mayas. Cristina, mi hermana, ______________ en casa hoy porque ella ______________ enferma, ¡pobrecita! Nosotros ______________ tristes por ella.

W4-4 Verbos irregulares en la primera persona: *yo*. Complete este párrafo con la forma correcta del verbo entre paréntesis.

Los sábados por la noche, yo siempre ______________ (salir) con mis amigos. Yo ______________ (estar) muy contenta cuando estoy con ellos. Yo ______________ (conocer) a muchas personas en Antigua, pero ______________ (saber) que mis amigos son las mejores personas de la ciudad. A veces yo ______________ (dar) fiestas en casa. Otras veces yo ______________ (hacer) mi tarea en casa con una amiga. Si voy a la casa de mi amiga Josefina, yo siempre ______________ (traer) algo para comer. Si estudiamos en mi casa, yo siempre ______________ (poner) un poco de música.

W4-5 *¿Saber o conocer?* Lea las siguientes oraciones y subraye *(underline)* la forma correcta de **saber** o **conocer** según el contexto. Después, escriba la forma correcta del verbo en el espacio en blanco.

Ejemplo: Yo *sé* hablar un poco de inglés. (saber / conocer)

1. Ahora, Rodrigo y Teresa ______________ a Ileana. (saber / conocer)
2. Tú ______________ bien Guatemala. (saber / conocer)
3. Cristina ______________ restaurantes de comida típica. (saber / conocer)
4. Nosotros ______________ mucho sobre el Tikal. (saber / conocer)

W4-6 *¿Saber o conocer?* Llene los espacios en blanco con la forma correcta de **saber** o **conocer.**

¿Ileana, ______________ a mi hermana mayor, Cristina? Ella es de aquí, pero ______________ muchos países latinoamericanos y ______________ hablar inglés y un poco de francés. Cristina es una persona muy activa. Trabaja, estudia, ______________ muchos restaurantes y además ______________ preparar comida guatemalteca muy bien. También es una buena hermana.

Nombre _______________ Fecha _______________

W4-7 Adverbios: Mis actividades. Conteste las siguientes preguntas sobre sus actividades. Use las palabras de la lista a continuación.

a veces	frecuentemente	normalmente	todos los días
todas las semanas	muchas veces	nunca	un poco
casi siempre	muy poco	siempre	

1. ¿Con qué frecuencia estudia usted español?

____

2. ¿Con qué frecuencia sale usted con sus amigos?

____

3. ¿Con qué frecuencia escribe usted en una computadora?

____

4. ¿Con qué frecuencia come usted comida guatemalteca?

____

5. ¿Con qué frecuencia habla usted con su familia?

____

Cultura

W4-8 ¿Verdadero o falso? Decida si las siguientes oraciones son verdaderas **(V)**, falsas **(F)** o si no hay suficiente información **(N)** para contestar.

1. _____ No es común tener varias generaciones en la misma casa.
2. _____ Los abuelos viven con sus hijos y nietos muchas veces.
3. _____ Muchos niños reciben nombres de santos.
4. _____ No es común tener más de una persona en la familia con el mismo nombre.
5. _____ Memo es un sobrenombre para Guillermo.
6. _____ Los hispanos tienen dos apellidos.

Nombre ______________________ Fecha ______________

¡A leer!: La leyenda del quetzal

Antes de leer

The **quetzal** is a beautiful and colorful bird that is the national symbol of Guatemala. It is also the name of its monetary currency, and it represents the spirit of freedom for the indigenous people.

Cognates **(Cognados)** *are words that are identical or very similar in spelling and meaning in English and in Spanish. Scan the legend below and see if you can find some.*

W4-9 Escriba los cognados de la lectura.

____

____

____

Vamos a leer

W4-10 Lea el artículo sobre el quetzal.

La leyenda del quetzal

El quetzal es uno de los pájaros *(birds)* más hermosos *(beautiful)* y raros del mundo. El quetzal es el emblema nacional de Guatemala. Tiene plumas *(feathers)* de colores brillantes. Sus plumas son rojas, verdes y azules, y tiene una cola *(tail)* muy bonita de tres pies de largo *(three feet long)*. Este pájaro es un símbolo religioso para los indígenas mayas y representa el espíritu de la libertad. El quetzal no puede vivir en cautiverio *(captivity)*. La imagen del quetzal aparece en las estampillas y en la moneda de Guatemala.

Después de leer

W4-11 Conteste las preguntas sobre la leyenda.

1. ¿Cuál es la idea principal *(main idea)* de "La leyenda del quetzal"?

   ____

2. ¿Qué es un quetzal?

   ____

3. ¿Qué representa el quetzal para los indígenas mayas?

   ____

Nombre ______________________ Fecha ____________

¡A escribir!

Antes de escribir

W4-12 Entreviste a un(a) compañero(a) de clase e incluya la siguiente información.

Remember to formulate questions in Spanish to ask for this information! Write your notes in the space below.

1. Estado civil ______________________
2. Número de hijos que tiene ______________________
3. Nombres de tres de las personas de su familia y las actividades preferidas de estas personas

   Persona #1: Nombre: ____________ Actividades: ____________ ____________

   Persona #2: Nombre: ____________ Actividades: ____________ ____________

   Persona #3: Nombre: ____________ Actividades: ____________ ____________
4. ¿Con qué frecuencia practican estas actividades? ¿Qué días de la semana?

   ____

   ____

   ____

> **Phrases:** describing people
> **Vocabulary:** days of the week; family members; leisure; time expressions; time of day
> **Grammar:** adverbs; adverbs ending in ***-mente***

Vamos a escribir

W4-13 Escriba un párrafo sobre su compañero(a) de clase, su familia y sus actividades favoritas. Siga el ejemplo.

Ejemplo: *Hay tres personas en la familia de Nicholas: Nicholas, su esposa Mary y su hija, Kelly. Nicholas tiene cuarenta y un años y es una persona activa. Le gusta hacer ejercicio. Todos los días por la mañana corre en el parque con su perro, Ralph. Su esposa, Mary, es una persona más tranquila. A ella le gusta leer el periódico y tomar café por la mañana. Su hija, Kelly, es una persona activa como su papá. Por la tarde ella ayuda a su mamá a preparar la comida. Después, va al centro con sus amigas. Luego Kelly hace su tarea en la computadora, mira televisión un poco y habla por teléfono con su novio.*

Después de escribir

W4-14 Haga un círculo alrededor de todos los verbos que usted usó en el párrafo. Subraye los sujetos. ¿Concuerdan *(Do . . . agree)* los verbos con los sujetos? Si no, haga las correcciones necesarias.

Nombre ______________________ Fecha ____________

Actividades y ejercicios orales

Pronunciación esencial

Linking words

Spanish speakers do not pronounce words as isolated elements. Instead, they link words together without interrupting the flow of sound.

CD1-29 **W4-15** A final consonant is linked with the initial vowel of the next word. Two identical consonants coming together are pronounced as a lengthened one. Listen to each sentence and repeat after the speaker.

In this conversation, Luis and Ileana speak to each other by linking words.

—Luis, ¿Qué vamos a hacer hoy?

—Bueno, Ileana, tenemos muchas cosas que hacer. Tenemos que ir a la Ciudad de Guatemala, a la ciudad de Antigua, al lago de Atitlán...

—Sí, pero necesitamos descansar... estoy cansada. ¿No estás cansado, Luis?

—No, no estoy cansado. ¿Dónde quieres descansar... aquí en mi casa o en el hotel?

—Quiero descansar + aquí en tu casa.

—¡Estás + en tu casa!

CD1-30 **W4-16** A final vowel is linked with the initial vowel of the next word. Two or more identical vowels coming together are pronounced as one. Listen to each sentence and repeat after the speaker.

—Tomás, voy + a + ir a la reunión sobre + ecoturismo a las siete. ¿Quieres ir?

—Sí, Luis, quiero + ir. ¿Sobre qué va + a hablar el director del hotel esta noche?

—Sobre la + hotelería *(hotel business)* en la zona del Tikal. Va + a ser interesante.

—¡Creo que sí! ¡Ya sabemos qué + importante son los hoteles para + el turismo *(tourism)*.

En contexto

CD1-31 **W4-17** **¡Tenemos muchas cosas que hacer!** Escuche la siguiente conversación. Decida si las oraciones son verdaderas **(V)**, falsas **(F)** o si no hay suficiente información **(N)** para contestar.

1. _____ Ileana viaja a Guatemala por primera vez.
2. _____ Tomás no conoce la Ciudad de Guatemala.
3. _____ Tomás no quiere visitar el Lago Atitlán.
4. _____ Tikal son ruinas de origen maya.
5. _____ Ileana va a ver las ruinas mañana.

Nombre ______________________________ Fecha ______________

VOCABULARIO ESENCIAL 

CD1-32 **W4-18 La familia de Luis Chávez.** Escuche la descripción de la familia de Luis y escriba el nombre de la persona que él describe debajo de cada dibujo.

1. ______________________

2. ______________________

3. ______________________

4. ______________________

5. ______________________

Nombre ______________________________ Fecha ______________

CD1-33 **W4-19 Las actividades de la familia Chávez.** Usted va a escuchar a doña Cristina Arzú de Chávez hablar de las actividades de su familia. Mientras usted escucha, escriba las actividades que hace cada persona.

Cristina ______________________________

Luis ______________________________

Rodrigo ______________________________

Nietos ______________________________

Nombre ______________________________ Fecha ______________

LECCIÓN 5 ¿QUÉ CARRERA QUIERES SEGUIR?

Cuaderno de ejercicios

VOCABULARIO ESENCIAL

W5-1 Las vidas profesionales. Escriba el nombre de cada profesión en el espacio debajo del dibujo indicado. Escoja de la lista a continuación. No va a necesitar todas las palabras.

trabajadora social	guías de turismo	programador
escritora	hombre de negocios	médica
músico	agentes de viajes	

1. ______________________

2. ______________________

3. ______________________

4. ______________________

5. ______________________

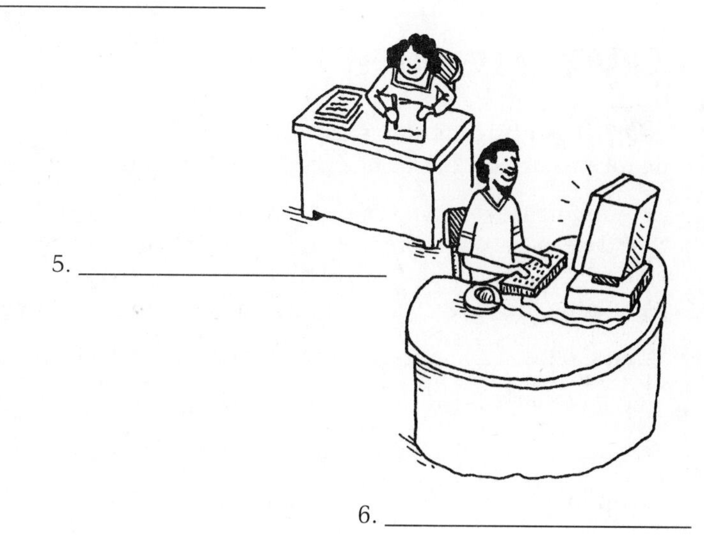

6. ______________________

Nombre ______________________________ Fecha ______________

W5-2 **¿Qué carrera sigue?** Escoja la respuesta más lógica.

1. _____ Una persona que estudia ciencias quiere ser...
   a. abogado(a).
   b. periodista.
   c. programador(a).
   d. científico(a).
2. _____ Una persona que trabaja en un hospital es...
   a. policía.
   b. médico(a).
   c. gerente.
   d. comerciante.
3. _____ Una persona que estudia periodismo quiere ser...
   a. investigador(a).
   b. abogado(a).
   c. oficinista.
   d. periodista.

W5-3 **¿Adónde voy?** Ileana no sabe adónde ir para las siguientes actividades. ¿Puede usted recomendarle a ella adónde puede ir? No necesita todas las palabras de la lista.

tienda por departamentos	hospital	agencia de viajes
restaurante	estación de policía	banco
librería de la universidad	laboratorio	

1. Para comprar libros, puedes ir a la ______________________________.
2. Si necesitas dinero, puedes ir al ______________________________.
3. Si estás enferma, necesitas ir al ______________________________.
4. ¿Vas de viaje? ¿Quieres el número de mi ______________________________?
5. En caso de un robo *(theft)*, hay que ir a la ______________________________.
6. Si necesitas comprar ropa y zapatos *(clothing and shoes)*, puedes ir a la

   ______________________________.

GRAMÁTICA ESENCIAL

W5-4 **Las obligaciones y los deseos de Ileana y sus amigos.** Llene los espacios en blanco con la forma correcta del verbo apropiado de la lista siguiente.

almorzar	pensar	tener	pedir	querer
desear	preferir	decir	poder	volver

Esta tarde, Ileana ______________ que hablar con sus tíos sobre el ecoturismo en el Pacífico. Ahora, ellos ______________ en el restaurante de los padres de Ileana. Su mamá ______________ que los frijoles negros son muy buenos aquí. Ileana ______________ que el arroz con leche *(rice pudding)* es el mejor del mundo y Tomás ______________ que el café es el mejor también. Después de almorzar, ______________ a casa y aquí ______________ mirar el juego de fútbol. Luis y Tomás también ______________ descansar mirando el juego.

Nombre ______________________ Fecha ____________

W5-5 Diálogo. Ileana está hablando con María Elena, una amiga de San José. Llene los espacios en blanco con la forma correcta del verbo apropiado de la lista siguiente.

comenzar	poder	seguir	volver
pensar	preferir	venir	

Ileana: ¿Cuándo ____________ ustedes a las clases de la universidad de San José?

María Elena: El lunes ____________ la universidad.

Ileana: ¿Qué carrera ____________ tú?

María Elena: Yo ____________ ser médica.

Ileana: Ah, por eso estudias medicina. ¿ ____________ tú trabajar como voluntaria en el hospital este semestre?

María Elena: Sí. Pero ____________ trabajar en la sala de emergencias porque es muy interesante.

W5-6 Preguntas personales. Conteste las siguientes preguntas con oraciones completas.

1. ¿Trabaja usted? ¿Dónde?

   ____

2. ¿A qué hora comienza a trabajar? Si no trabaja, ¿a qué hora comienza a estudiar?

   ____

3. ¿Dónde prefiere almorzar?

   ____

4. ¿Qué tiene que hacer hoy?

   ____

5. ¿Qué piensa hacer mañana?

   ____

6. ¿A qué hora vuelve a su casa hoy?

   ____

W5-7 ¿Qué están haciendo estas personas? Describa con oraciones completas lo que están haciendo las personas indicadas. Cambie las palabras o agregue *(add)* más palabras cuando sea necesario.

1. Tomás / viajar a / San José

   ____

2. la señora Gamboa / enseñar / a cocinar *(to cook)* / el restaurante

   ____

3. Alejandro / volver / casa

   ____

4. el señor Gamboa / servir / comida / el restaurante

   ____

W5-8 Una familia ocupada. ¿Qué están haciendo Ileana, su familia y sus amigos a la hora indicada?

Ejemplo: Ileana habla con sus amigos. (12:00 p.m.)
Ileana está hablando con sus amigos a las doce del día.

1. La señora Gamboa trabaja en el restaurante. (8:00 a.m.)

   ____

2. El señor Gamboa estudia la contabilidad del restaurante. (9:00 a.m.)

   ____

3. Ileana y sus amigos almuerzan en el Café Tico. (12:00 p.m.)

   ____

4. Sara prepara la información turística para Ileana. (2:00 p.m.)

   ____

5. Alejandro mira las noticias sobre el Parque Nacional de Santa Rosa. (4:00 p.m.)

   ____

Cultura

W5-9 En la universidad. Lea las siguientes oraciones y escriba la letra de la respuesta correcta en el espacio en blanco.

1. ____ Before students in Latin America and Spain can enroll in a university, they must complete...
   a. college.
   b. primary.
   c. secondary.

2. ____ Competition for acceptance in government-run universities is intense because...
   a. everyone can enroll.
   b. students must pass rigorous entrance exams.
   c. many students enter the labor force instead of going to the university.

3. ____ Most students live...
   a. in residence halls.
   b. in boardinghouses or in their parents' homes.
   c. in their own apartments.

4. ____ The administrations of most universities in Spanish-speaking countries...
   a. can determine their own policies.
   b. receive direction from the government.
   c. answer to policies set by the voting public.

Nombre ______________________ Fecha ____________

¡A leer!: Los anuncios clasificados

Antes de leer

Vocabulario

los beneficios benefits	**la dirección** address
los requisitos requirements	**el puesto** job, position

W5-10 Muchas compañías buscan personal y ponen anuncios en la sección de anuncios clasificados de un periódico. Indique el orden en que aparece normalmente la siguiente información.

1. ____	a. los beneficios del puesto
2. ____	b. los requisitos para el puesto
3. ____	c. el nombre de la compañía o empresa
4. ____	d. la dirección de la compañía
5. ____	e. el número de teléfono de la compañía
6. ____	f. el nombre del puesto

Vamos a leer

W5-11 Mire los seis anuncios del periódico *La Nación* de San José, Costa Rica, aquí y en la página siguiente y complete el cuadro a continuación con la información indicada.

	Puesto anunciado	Compañía/empresa	Requisito para el puesto	Sueldo
1.	____	____	____	____
2.	____	____	____	____
3.	____	____	____	____
4.	____	____	____	____
5.	____	____	____	____
6.	____	____	____	____

Nombre ______________________ Fecha ______________

EMPRESA TURISTICA

requiere

ADMINISTRADOR

en nuevo desarrollo en el Pacífico

Requisitos:

- Mayor de 25 años, con experiencia en hotelería y turismo, dispuesto a residir la mayor parte del tiempo en la zona. Requisito mínimo idioma inglés, preferiblemente con otro idioma adicional.
- Conocimientos básicos de pesca y lanchas.

Interesados enviar currículum y foto reciente al apartado 1373–1000, San José.

(2.)

COSTA RICA DENTAL & MEDICAL SUPPLY CO.

Dr. M. Fischel Co. S. A

REQUIERE:

SECRETARIA EJECUTIVA BILINGÜE

Requisitos:

- Grado académico que la capacite para el desempeño del puesto.
- Inglés fluido, tanto oral como escrito
- Carácter y disposición para trabajar bajo presión
- Excelente presentación
- Buen trato personal
- Destrezas en el uso de télex, fax y microcomputadoras

Se ofrece:

- Salarios a convenir
- Magnífico ambiente de trabajo
- Estabilidad laboral
- Asociación solidarista
- Otros beneficios.

Interesados favor enviar currículum vitae, con fotografía reciente y pretensiones salariales al Apdo. 434–1000, San José Depto. Reqrsos Humanos.

EMPRESA NACIONAL

requiere los servicios de

QUIMICO

Requisitos:

- Licenciado en Química
- Incorporado al colegio respectivo
- Dispuesto a residir en Guápiles
- Deseable experiencia mínima de un año en análisis químicos de suelos y plantas

Se ofrece:

- Estabilidad laboral
- Excelente ambiente de trabajo
- Asociación solidarista
- Médico de empresa

Los interesados deberán presentar su currículum vitae a más tardar el día 10-01-90, incluyendo fotocopias de los títulos, fotografía reciente y pretensiones de salario al apartado 1859–1000, San José.

Nota: No se considerarán solicitudes incompletas.

(4.)

COMPAÑIA EXPORTADORA EN EXPANSION

requiere los servicios de un

CONTADOR

Requisitos:

1. Amplia experiencia en contabilidad
2. Incorporado al colegio respectivo
3. Experiencia en trámites bancarios de exportación
4. Conocimiento del sistema computadorizado de contabilidad
5. Amplia disposición para el trabajo

Ofrecemos agradable ambiente de trabajo, incentivos y salario acorde con el puesto.

Interesados favor concertar cita al teléfono 55–29–92 en horas de oficina.

PARKE-DAVIS

solicita los servicios profesionales de

DOS VISITADORES MEDICOS

que reúnan los siguientes requisitos:

Profesión:	Farmacéutico–a (graduado) (a)
Vehículo:	Modelo reciente – buen estado
Edad:	25–35 años
Experiencia:	Preferencia con experiencia en visita médica
Otros:	Buena presentación, relaciones humanas, deseo de trabajar y progresar
Se ofrece:	Salario base Bonos sobre ventas Depreciación vehículo Gasolina – viáticos y 55% seguro vehículo.

Interesados enviar currículum a Dismercasa de Costa Rica, S.A. Barrio La Pitahaya, de Pollos Kentucky en el Paseo Colón 500 metros al norte y 125 al este, o apartado postal: 6–2100, Guadalupe.

REQUIERE LOS SERVICIOS DE

UN INGENIERO INDUSTRIAL

REQUISITOS:

Preferiblemente con experiencia en programación de la producción y operación de equipo de cómputo sencillo.

SE OFRECE:

Salario según capacidad
Magníficas condiciones de trabajo
Oportunidad de desarrollo

Interesados enviar currículum vitae al apartado 2000–1000 San José a: INGENIERO INDUSTRIAL.

Después de leer

W5-12 Usted busca un(a) programador(a) de computadoras para su compañía. Escriba un anuncio para el periódico. Incluya 1. el nombre, la dirección y el número de teléfono de su compañía, 2. el nombre del puesto, 3. los requisitos para el puesto, 4. el sueldo que se ofrece, 5. los beneficios que se ofrecen y 6. otra información necesaria.

____

____

____

____

____

____

____

¡A escribir!

Antes de escribir

W5-13 Conteste las siguientes preguntas con oraciones completas.

1. ¿Qué carrera sigue usted?

   ____

2. ¿Qué clases toma usted para esta carrera?

   ____

   ____

3. ¿Qué otras clases necesita tomar usted en el futuro?

   ____

   ____

4. ¿Qué sueldo quiere usted?

   ____

5. ¿Dónde quiere trabajar?

   ____

Vocabulary: professions; studies; trades
Grammar: accents; general rules; verbs; gerund, **poder,** progressive tenses

Vamos a escribir

W5-14 Escriba un párrafo sobre sus planes para su carrera futura. Incluya la información de las preguntas anteriores *(above)* y agregue otra información cuando sea necesario.

____

____

____

____

____

____

____

____

Después de escribir

W5-15 Intercambie el párrafo de arriba con el de un(a) compañero(a) de clase. Examine el párrafo de su compañero(a) para ver si todos los acentos están bien puestos. Si una palabra lleva acento y no lo tiene, agrégueselo. Si una palabra no debe llevar acento pero lo tiene, bórreselo *(erase it)*.

Nombre ______________________________ Fecha ______________

Actividades y ejercicios orales

Pronunciación esencial

Spanish *j* and *g*

CD1-34 **W5-16** Spanish **j** has a sound somewhat like the *h* in *hill,* but harder. It is never pronounced like the English *j* of *jet*. Listen to the following sentences and repeat after the speaker.

—¿Traba**j**a Tomás el **j**ueves por la tarde?
—Sí, Ileana. Ese *(That)* **j**oven es muy traba**j**ador.
—¿Cuándo va a **j**ugar al fútbol con sus amigos?
—Siempre **j**uega los domingos.

CD1-35 **W5-17** Spanish **g** before an **e** or **i** is pronounced like the Spanish **j.** Listen to each sentence and repeat after the speaker.

—¿Cómo se llama tu hijo, José?
—Se llama Jor**g**e.
—Jor**g**e vive en Guatemala, ¿no?
—Sí, estudia in**g**eniería allí.
—¿Es ingeli**g**ente tu Jor**g**e?
—Sí. Va a ser un in**g**eniero in**g**enioso *(ingenious)*.

CD1-36 **W5-18** In all other cases, **g** is pronounced approximately like the *g* in *go*. Listen to each sentence and repeat after the speaker.

—Yolanda, éste es mi ami**g**o **G**ustavo **G**onzález.
—Mucho **g**usto, **G**ustavo.
—El **g**usto es mío, Yolanda.

Spanish *h*

CD1-37 **W5-19** Spanish **h** is never pronounced. Listen to the following sentences and repeat after the speaker.

—**H**ija, ¿qué estás **h**aciendo?
—Estoy **h**ablando con mi **h**ermano por teléfono, mamá.

En contexto

CD1-38 **W5-20** **¡Pura vida!** Escuche la siguiente conversación. Decida si las siguientes oraciones son verdaderas **(V)**, falsas **(F)** o si no hay suficiente información **(N)** para contestar.

1. _____ Son las dos de la tarde; es hora de beber algo.
2. _____ Ileana quiere café con leche.
3. _____ Tomás quiere café con leche.
4. _____ Después, ellos van a una agencia de viajes.
5. _____ A Luis le gusta la idea de ir a una agencia de viajes.

Nombre ______________________ Fecha ____________

VOCABULARIO ESENCIAL

CD1-39 **W5-21 Los amigos de Ileana.** Ileana va a hablar de sus amigos Luis y Tomás. Escuche a Ileana y escriba la información apropiada en los espacios indicados.

1. ¿Cómo son Luis y Tomás?

   ____

2. ¿Son casados o solteros?

   ____

3. ¿Qué estudian Luis, Ileana y Tomás?

   ____

4. ¿Dónde estudian?

   ____

5. ¿Qué quieren hacer ellos en San José?

   ____

Nombre ______________________ Fecha ______________

LECCIÓN 6 ¡HACE MUCHO CALOR EN PANAMÁ!

Cuaderno de ejercicios

VOCABULARIO ESENCIAL

W6-1 **¿Qué tiempo hace?** Describa el tiempo que hace en los siguientes dibujos e indique qué temporada es. Hay más dibujos en la página 58.

1. Estación: Primavera
   Tiempo: Hace sol
   ¿Tienes sed? quizas (maybe)

2. Estación: El verano
   Tiempo: Hace calor
   ¿Tienes calor? tengo calor

3. Estación: El otoño
   Tiempo: Hace fresco
   ¿Tienes calor? No tengo calor

4. Estación: El inverano
   Tiempo: Hace much frio y está nevando
   ¿Tienes frío? si tengo frio.

Nombre ______________________ Fecha ______________

5. Tiempo: Esta muy nublado

¿Tienes calor? No, tengo frio.

6. Tiempo: Esta lloviendo

¿Tienes frío? No tengo frio

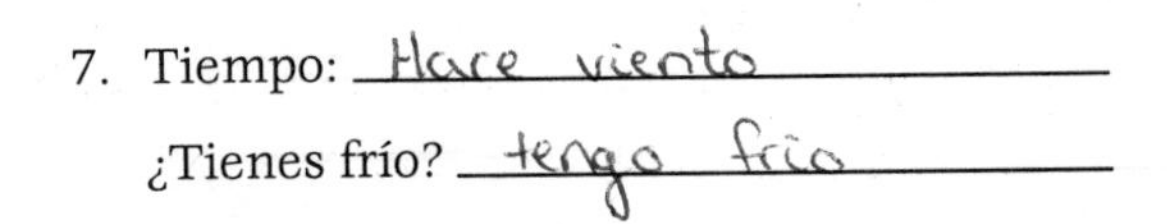

7. Tiempo: Hace viento

¿Tienes frío? tengo frio

W6-2 **¿Cuánto es?** El señor Gamboa tiene que escribir cheques para pagar las cuentas *(bills)* del restaurante. Ayúdele a escribir el número de cada cheque.

Ejemplo: $300
trescientos

1. $ 198 ______________________
2. $ 420 ______________________
3. $ 541 ______________________
4. $ 399 ______________________
5. $1.524 ______________________
6. $1.999 ______________________

Nombre ______________________________ Fecha ______________

Gramática esencial

W6-3 La rutina de todos los días. Complete las siguientes oraciones con la forma correcta de los verbos entre paréntesis.

Ejemplo: Tomás *se despierta* a las 6:00. (despertarse)
¿A qué hora *te despiertas* tú?
Yo *me despierto a las 7:00.*

1. Ileana ______________ a las once de la noche. (acostarse)

   ¿A qué hora ______________ tú?

   Yo ______________.

2. A veces Luis ______________ con dificultad. (dormirse)

   ¿______________ tú fácilmente o con dificultad?

   Yo ______________.

3. Alejandro ______________ a las siete. (levantarse)

   ¿A qué hora ______________ tú?

   Yo ______________.

4. La señora Gamboa ______________ y el señor Gamboa ______________. (bañarse / ducharse)

   ¿Qué prefieres, ______________ o ______________ por la mañana?

   Yo ______________.

5. Tía Sara ______________ elegantemente para ir a trabajar los lunes. (vestirse)

   ¿Cómo ______________ tú los lunes?

   Yo ______________.

W6-4 ¿Qué pasó ayer? Lea los siguientes párrafos y luego cambie los verbos al pretérito para expresar lo que pasó ayer con los amigos.

Hoy Tomás se levanta a las 5:00, se lava los dientes, se afeita y se ducha. Luego se viste y toma café con leche. A las 6:00 llama a Luis e Ileana al hotel para despertarlos.

Luis e Ileana se levantan también. Se bañan, se visten y esperan a Tomás en el hotel. A la 1:00 ellos vuelven al hotel, descansan un poco y luego almuerzan. A las 2:00 vuelven a la oficina de ecoturismo y trabajan hasta las 6:00 de la tarde.

Tomás invita a Ileana y a Luis a cenar en el restaurante El Pacífico. Luis e Ileana comen muy bien. Ellos beben café panameño.

Ayer, ______________________________

____

____

____

____

____

____

____

____

____

____

____

____

____

____

____

____

W6-5 **¿Qué hicieron ayer?** Describa con oraciones en el pasado lo que hicieron varias personas. Cambie las palabras y agregue más palabras cuando sea necesario.

Ejemplo: Ileana / cenar con sus amigos anoche
Ileana cenó con sus amigos anoche.

1. Luis / salir a tomar una cerveza

____

2. Tomás / comprar regalos para sus parientes

____

3. el señor Gamboa / servir comida en el restaurante

____

4. Ileana / hablar con su mamá

____

5. la señora Gamboa / volver al restaurante por la tarde

____

Cultura

W6-6 **¿Dónde estoy?** Escoja la mejor respuesta para las siguientes preguntas.

1. _____ Las estaciones del año en el hemisferio norte son... al hemisferio sur.
   a. iguales
   b. un poco más frías
   c. opuestas
2. _____ Los latinoamericanos usan... para medir *(to measure)* la temperatura.
   a. gafas de radio-X
   b. grados centígrados
   c. grados bajo cero
3. _____ Tu comida tiene muchísimo chile. Tú dices:...
   a. ¡Ay! ¡Qué caliente!
   b. ¡Ay! ¿Dónde está mi madre?
   c. ¡Ay! ¡Qué picante!

Nombre ______________________________ Fecha ______________

¡A leer!: El pronóstico del tiempo

Antes de leer

W6-7 Haga una lista de las expresiones que conoces en español para expresar qué tiempo hace.

______________________ ______________________ ______________________

______________________ ______________________ ______________________

______________________ ______________________ ______________________

Vamos a leer

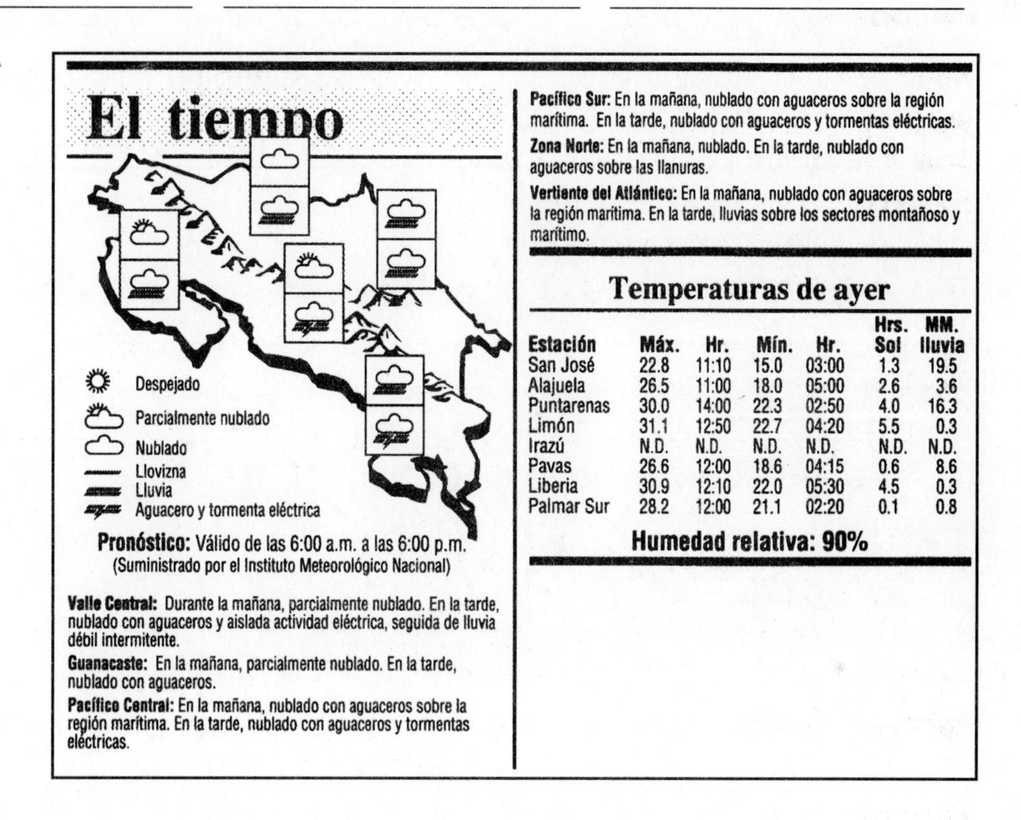

El tiempo

Despejado
Parcialmente nublado
Nublado
Llovizna
Lluvia
Aguacero y tormenta eléctrica

Pronóstico: Válido de las 6:00 a.m. a las 6:00 p.m.
(Suministrado por el Instituto Meteorológico Nacional)

Valle Central: Durante la mañana, parcialmente nublado. En la tarde, nublado con aguaceros y aislada actividad eléctrica, seguida de lluvia débil intermitente.

Guanacaste: En la mañana, parcialmente nublado. En la tarde, nublado con aguaceros.

Pacífico Central: En la mañana, nublado con aguaceros sobre la región marítima. En la tarde, nublado con aguaceros y tormentas eléctricas.

Pacífico Sur: En la mañana, nublado con aguaceros sobre la región marítima. En la tarde, nublado con aguaceros y tormentas eléctricas.

Zona Norte: En la mañana, nublado. En la tarde, nublado con aguaceros sobre las llanuras.

Vertiente del Atlántico: En la mañana, nublado con aguaceros sobre la región marítima. En la tarde, lluvias sobre los sectores montañoso y marítimo.

Temperaturas de ayer

Estación	Máx.	Hr.	Mín.	Hr.	Hrs. Sol	MM. lluvia
San José	22.8	11:10	15.0	03:00	1.3	19.5
Alajuela	26.5	11:00	18.0	05:00	2.6	3.6
Puntarenas	30.0	14:00	22.3	02:50	4.0	16.3
Limón	31.1	12:50	22.7	04:20	5.5	0.3
Irazú	N.D.	N.D.	N.D.	N.D.	N.D.	N.D.
Pavas	26.6	12:00	18.6	04:15	0.6	8.6
Liberia	30.9	12:10	22.0	05:30	4.5	0.3
Palmar Sur	28.2	12:00	21.1	02:20	0.1	0.8

Humedad relativa: 90%

W6-8 Use los símbolos y el mapa de Costa Rica para escribir el pronóstico del tiempo *(weather report)* para las siguientes regiones. Esta actividad continuá en la página 62.

1. Complete las listas que aparecen a continuación.

	Por la mañana	Por la tarde
Región central del Pacífico	______________	______________
Región sur del Pacífico	______________	______________
Zona norte	______________	______________
Valle central	______________	______________
Vertiente del Atlántico	______________	______________

2. ¿En qué regiones no llueve por la mañana?

____

3. ¿En qué regiones hay tormentas eléctricas por la tarde?

____

W6-9 Mire la tabla de las temperaturas de ayer en Costa Rica.

1. ¿Las temperaturas de Costa Rica son en grados centígrados o Fahrenheit?
2. ¿Cuáles fueron las temperaturas máximas y mínimas en San José?

Después de leer

W6-10 Escriba el pronóstico del tiempo para la región donde usted vive. Puede dibujar un mapa y usar los símbolos del tiempo para reportar el clima.

MAPA

____
____
____
____
____
____
____
____
____
____
____
____

Nombre ______________________ Fecha ______________

¡A escribir!

Antes de escribir

W6-11 Conteste las siguientes preguntas que le hace un amigo sobre lo que usted hace todos los días.

1. ¿A qué hora te levantas?
   ____
2. ¿Te bañas por la mañana?
   ____
3. ¿Te gusta peinarte?
   ____
4. ¿Te afeitas? ¿Te maquillas?
   ____
5. ¿A qué hora vas al trabajo? ¿Dónde trabajas?
   ____
6. ¿A qué hora llegas a tu primera clase?
   ____
7. ¿Tienes hambre a las doce del día? ¿Dónde almuerzas?
   ____
8. ¿A qué hora cenas? ¿Qué comes para la cena?
   ____
9. ¿Qué haces por la noche?
   ____
10. ¿Qué haces antes de acostarte?
   ____
11. ¿Qué bebes cuando tienes sed a medianoche?
   ____

Phrases: sequencing events; talking about daily routines
Vocabulary: leisure; studies; time of day
Grammar: adverb types; adverbs ending in **-mente;** verbs; present, preterite, reflexives

Nombre ______________________ Fecha ______________

Vamos a escribir

W6-12 Usando la información anterior, escriba un ensayo sobre su rutina diaria. Incluya todos los detalles necesarios.

Ejemplo: *Todos los días me despierto a las cinco y media de la mañana, pero no me levanto hasta las cinco y cuarenta y cinco. Me baño rápidamente porque tengo que ir a trabajar a las seis y media. No me gusta peinarme ni maquillarme porque toma mucho tiempo.*

Siempre salgo para mi trabajo tarde y llego a las siete y quince todos los días. Trabajo en un restaurante por la mañana donde el cliente siempre tiene razón. Termino de trabajar a la una, pero siempre tengo hambre al mediodía y almuerzo en el restaurante antes de salir para la universidad.

Por la tarde tengo dos clases. Mi clase de biología comienza a las dos. Es una clase interesante. A las cinco y media tengo mi clase de español. El profesor es muy divertido e interesante.

Vuelvo a mi casa a las siete y media y miro televisión y preparo la cena. Me gusta mirar el pronóstico del tiempo todas las noches. Después de cenar, estudio y escucho música. Me acuesto a las doce después de tomar un refresco, lavarme los dientes y la cara y ponerme el pijama.

Ahora, escriba usted sobre su propia vida diaria en otra hoja de papel.

Después de escribir

W6-13 Escriba el ensayo otra vez en el pasado. Agregue o cambie la información cuando sea necesario.

Look carefully at the model paragraph written in the past. Not all verbs have been changed to the past tense. The verbs that state what the speaker does routinely appear in the present tense. Only the verbs that describe a completed past action are in the past.

Ejemplo: *Ayer me desperté a las cinco y media de la mañana, pero no me levanté hasta las cinco y cuarenta y cinco. Me bañé rápidamente porque siempre tengo que ir a trabajar a las seis y media. No me peiné ni me maquillé porque toma mucho tiempo.*

Salí para mi trabajo tarde y llegué a las siete y quince de la mañana. Trabajo en un restaurante por la mañana donde el cliente siempre tiene razón. Terminé de trabajar a la una. Tenía hambre (I was hungry) *y almorcé en el restaurante antes de salir para la universidad.*

Por la tarde tuve (had) *dos clases. Mi clase de biología comienza a las dos.* ***Fue*** *muy interesante. A las cinco y media* ***fui*** *a mi clase de español y estudié mucho.*

Volví a casa a las siete y media y miré televisión y preparé la cena. Miré el pronóstico del tiempo, como todas las noches. Después de cenar, estudié y escuché música. Me acosté a las doce después de tomar un refresco, lavarme los dientes y la cara y ponerme el pijama.

Fue =** ***preterite of **ser;** ***presented in Lección 7***
Fui =** ***preterit of **ir;** ***presented in Lección 7***

W6-14 Haga una lista de todos los verbos y sujetos de sus dos ensayos. ¿Concuerdan los sujetos con los verbos?

Presente		Pasado	
Sujeto	**Verbo**	**Sujeto**	**Verbo**
______	______	______	______
______	______	______	______
______	______	______	______
______	______	______	______
______	______	______	______

Actividades y ejercicios orales

PRONUNCIACIÓN ESENCIAL

Spanish *d*

Spanish **d** has two sounds, depending on its position within a word or a phrase.

CD1-40 **W6-15** At the beginning of a phrase or a sentence, or after **l** or **n**, Spanish **d** is pronounced like English *d* in *dance,* but somewhat softer. Listen to the following sentences and repeat after the speaker.

—**D**iego, ¿qué estás hacien**d**o?
—¡Ah, Raquel! Estoy leyen**d**o una carta.
—¿**D**e quién?
—Es de **D**aniel **D**urán.
—¿**D**ónde vive **D**aniel ahora?
—En **D**urango, México. Tiene trabajo allí.
—¡Qué bien!

CD1-41 **W6-16** In all other positions, especially between vowels, Spanish **d** is pronounced like the *th* in *then.* Listen to the following sentences and repeat after the speaker.

—¡Hola, Tomás! ¿Qué tal?
—Estoy cansa**d**o, Ileana. El trabajo **d**e la oficina es muy **d**uro.
—Luis está preocupa**d**o por ti. Piensa que **d**ebes pasear con nosotros.
—Debo trabajar, pero **d**ebo pasear también. ¡Tienen razón!

Spanish *r* and *rr*

CD1-42 **W6-17** Spanish **r** is pronounced like the *d* sound in the sentence *Betty had a little bitty kitty.* Listen to the following sentences and repeat after the speaker.

—Luis e Ileana, ¿quie**r**en cena**r** aho**r**a?
—Sí, Tomás, g**r**acias. Pe**r**o, ¿tenemos que camina**r**?
—Sí, pe**r**o el luga**r** está ce**r**ca, a veinte minutos.
—¡Pe**r**fecto! Vamos a camina**r** y a hace**r** eje**r**cicio.

CD1-43 **W6-18** In Spanish, **rr** is pronounced like the single **r,** but the tongue bounces several times against the ridge behind the upper teeth. The **rr** is trilled somewhat like a child imitating the sound of a motor. The single **r** is also trilled when it begins a word, and within a word after **l, n,** or **s.** Listen to the following sentences and repeat after the speaker.

—Estoy abu**rr**ido, Luis. Quiero caminar **r**ápido.
—Vamos al restaurante.
—Sí, vamos. Allí viene un pe**rr**o que co**rr**e **r**ápido.
—A mí no me gustan los pe**rr**os.

Nombre ______________________________ Fecha ______________

En contexto

CD1-44 **W6-19** **¡Hace mucho sol en Panamá!** Escuche la siguiente conversación. Decida si las siguientes oraciones son verdaderas **(V)**, falsas **(F)** o si no hay suficiente información **(N)** para contestar.

1. _____ Ileana y Luis comenzaron el viaje a las seis de la mañana.
2. _____ Ellos almorzaron en el fuerte San Lorenzo.
3. _____ Ellos almorzaron muy bien.
4. _____ El almuerzo es bueno y económico.
5. _____ Ellos van a cenar en el restaurante Balboa esta noche.

Vocabulario esencial

CD1-45 **W6-20** **¿A cuánto está la temperatura?** Usted va a escuchar una descripción del tiempo en diferentes ciudades del mundo. Escriba la temperatura para cada ciudad.

Ciudad	**Tiempo**	**Temperatura**
Guatemala	*Hace buen tiempo*	*28° C, 84° F*
Acapulco	______________	______________
Barcelona	______________	______________
Moscú	______________	______________
Sydney	______________	______________

CD1-46 **6-21** **La rutina diaria.** Luis y Tomás están hablando de su rutina diaria. Lea las actividades que aparecen a continuación y póngalas en orden según la siguiente información.

La rutina de Tomás	**La rutina de Luis**
__*1*__ Se levanta.	_____ Se levanta.
_____ Se baña.	_____ Se baña.
_____ Se desayuna.	_____ Se desayuna.
_____ Se viste.	_____ Se viste.
_____ Se lava los dientes.	_____ Se lava los dientes.
_____ Se va a la oficina.	_____ Se va a la oficina.

PASO 3 ¡Buena onda!

LECCIÓN 7 ¡TENGO GANAS DE IR A LA PLAYA!

Cuaderno de ejercicios

VOCABULARIO ESENCIAL

W7-1 Deportes y pasatiempos. Ponga la letra de la actividad que se describe a continuación *(below)*.

1. ____ para escuchar música en vivo *(live)*
2. ____ para estar en el Internet
3. ____ para ser como Maradona o Pelé
4. ____ para estar en las montañas
5. ____ para ser como Sammy Sosa
6. ____ para ver el arte de Picasso, Dalí y Miró
7. ____ para ser como Michael Jordan
8. ____ para nadar en el mar
9. ____ para ver las obras de Shakespeare y Lope de Vega
10. ____ ser como Lance Armstrong

a. acampar en las montañas
b. ir a un concierto
c. ir a la playa
d. ir al teatro
e. navegar por la Red
f. visitar museos
g. montar en bicicleta
h. jugar al baloncesto
i. jugar al béisbol
j. jugar al fútbol

GRAMÁTICA ESENCIAL

W7-2 Una fiesta. ¿Qué pasó en la fiesta que hicieron los padres de Alicia para despedir *(to say good-bye)* a Alicia? Escriba oraciones completas, según el ejemplo.

Ejemplo: muchos amigos y parientes / ir a la fiesta
Muchos amigos y parientes fueron a la fiesta.

1. Alicia les / dar un abrazo a todos

____

2. la señora Benson / estar un poco enferma

____

3. algunos de los invitados / poder bailar toda la noche

____

4. el señor Benson / ir al supermercado donde / tener que comprar más refrescos

____

____

5. los amigos de Miguel y Shawn no / querer volver a casa

____

____

6. la tía Matilde / servir su famosa tortilla

____

____

7. muchos amigos de la universidad / venir a la fiesta y / traer cerveza fría

____

____

____

8. cuando los invitados irse / Alicia / ponerse el pijama, ella / sentirse muy cansada, entonces / acostarse y / dormirse

____

____

____

9. todos / decir que la fiesta / ser realmente maravillosa

____

____

W7-3 ¿Qué hicieron los Benson durante las vacaciones? Lea la siguiente narración de Alicia sobre las vacaciones y llene los espacios en blanco con la forma correcta del pretérito del verbo indicado.

El año pasado, nosotros ______________ (ir) al norte de Wisconson para esquiar. ______________ (Ser) muy divertido visitar esa zona. La noche antes de salir para el norte, todos nosotros ______________ (acostarse) temprano. Por la mañana mi mamá y yo ______________ (levantarse) a las cinco, y ______________ (ducharse) antes de despertar a los otros. Mi papá no ______________ (levantarse) hasta las seis y ______________ (ser) muy difícil levantarlo. Por fin, nosotros ______________ (salir) a las siete y ______________ (llegar) al norte temprano. Al día siguiente, Miguel y yo ______________ (ir) a esquiar. Mi mamá y Shawn ______________ (llegar) un poco más tarde porque ellos ______________ (tener) que desayunar primero. Shawn ______________ (sacar) fotos con su cámara nueva y ______________ (comprar) chocolates. A ver... ¿qué más ______________ (hacer) nosotros? Otro día ______________ (ver) una película estupenda en el cine. ______________ (Ir) a un concierto y ______________ (esquiar) mucho por todas las monañas. En fin ______________ (divertirse) mucho y lo ______________ (pasar) muy bien.

Nombre ______________________________ Fecha ______________

W7-4 Los pasatiempos y los deportes. Complete las siguientes oraciones lógicamente, indicando los pasatiempos y deportes apropiados para cada situación.

1. Cuando voy a la piscina, me gusta ______________________________.
2. En diciembre voy a Colorado. Cuando estoy allí, me gusta ______________________________.
3. Me gustan los animales, por eso, voy a ______________________________.
4. Me gusta mucho hacer ejercicio, por eso, cuando hace bueno tiempo, voy a ______________________________.

W7-5 Todos tenemos diferentes gustos. Mire las listas de personas, lugares y cosas que aparecen a continuación. Escriba lo que les gusta o no les gusta a las siguientes personas que usted conoce.

Lugares	**Cosas**
las islas tropicales	las frutas
las montañas	los regalos
los océanos	las grabadoras
los lugares *(places)* desérticos	los trajes de baño
los países europeos (sudamericanos, asiáticos)	los juegos electrónicos
los restaurantes étnicos (románticos)	las cintas de música rock/jazz/clásica
las universidades grandes (pequeñas)	los deportes acuáticos / de equipo
las ciudades modernas	las bebidas alcohólicas/frías/calientes

Ejemplos: *A mi papá le gustan los deportes de equipo.*
A mi papá no le gustan los restaurantes románticos.

1. A mi papá ______________________________.
2. A mi mamá ______________________________.
3. A mis compañeros de clase ______________________________.
4. A mi profesor(a) ______________________________.
5. A mi mejor amigo(a) y a mí ______________________________.
6. A mí ______________________________.

W7-6 Busca compañero(a). Mire la encuesta *(poll)* de abajo y decida si a usted le gustan las actividades de la lista. Si le gusta cierta actividad, escriba **sí** en el espacio indicado. Si no le gusta, escriba **no.** Luego entreviste a un(a) compañero(a) y escriba la respuesta en el espacio indicado.

Actividad	**¿Me gusta?**	**¿Te gusta?**
1. sacar fotos	________	________
2. jugar cartas	________	________
3. comer palomitas de maíz	________	________
4. ver un partido de fútbol	________	________
5. ir a la playa	________	________
6. esquiar	________	________
7. el submarinismo	________	________
8. los museos de arte moderno	________	________
9. comer helado de chocolate	________	________
10. montar en bicicleta	________	________

W7-7 A mí me gusta... Ahora escriba diez oraciones siguiendo el ejemplo a continuación.

Ejemplo: sacar fotos (nombre)
A mí me gusta sacar fotos, pero a Miguel no le gusta.

1. ______________________
2. ______________________
3. ______________________
4. ______________________
5. ______________________
6. ______________________
7. ______________________
8. ______________________
9. ______________________
10. ______________________

W7-8 *¿Por o para?* Ileana habla con Alicia sobre un examen en la clase de economía. Para completar la conversación, decida si es necesario poner **por** o **para** en el espacio.

Ileana: Alicia, ____________ favor, ¿puedo usar tu libro de economía?

Alicia: ¿Lo necesitas ____________ tu examen mañana, ¿no?

Ileana: Sí. Sólo quiero tu libro ____________ dos horas hoy ____________ la noche.

Alicia: Claro que sí. Yo te lo traigo ____________ las 6:00. ¿Vale?

Ileana: Ay, gracias ____________ todo, amiga.

CULTURA

W7-9 Deportes y pasatiempos en el mundo hispano. Conteste las siguientes preguntas según las lecturas de la **Lección 7.**

1. Es muy común participar en actividades... en el mundo hispano durante el tiempo libre.
   a. individuales
   b. peligrosas e ilegales
   c. sociales y familiares

2. Todos los países hispanos tienen un equipo nacional de...
   a. jugadores de universidades.
   b. fútbol.
   c. golf.

3. El béisbol es más popular en....
   a. el Brasil.
   b. España.
   c. el Caribe.

4. Hoy en el mundo hispano hay equipos deportivos...
   a. solamente para los hombres.
   b. solamente para los profesionales.
   c. para mujeres, hombres, profesionales y semiprofesionales.

5. Algunos entrenadores norteamericanos emplean a los mejores jugadores latinaoamericanos de béisbol y algunos entrenadores latinoamericanos emplean a los mejores jugadores americanos de...
   a. básquetbol.
   b. béisbol
   c. fútbol.
   d. golf.

¡A leer!: Submarinismo

Antes de leer

W7-10 Conteste las preguntas antes de leer el artículo.

Remember your scanning skills from earlier chapters . . . It may be helpful to look over the questions following the reading before beginning. That way, you can scan the article for the information you need and use that to guide you.

1. ¿Sabe usted algo de submarinismo?

______

2. ¿Le gustaría hacer submarinismo?

______

Vamos a leer

◆ SUBMARINISMO ◆

Si te atrae la idea de practicar un deporte de aventura y te gusta el mar, el submarinismo puede ser la mejor opción. Ahora es posible seguir un curso de iniciación que en sólo 2-3 semanas te permitirá hacer las primeras inmersiones. Este curso combina la formación teórica con las prácticas en piscina y mar. Al finalizar el curso obtendrás la titulación B1E (Buceador una estrella) de la FEDAS (Federación Española de Actividades Subacuáticas) y de la CMAS (Confederación Mundial de Actividades Subacuáticas), titulación que te permitirá bucear por todo el mundo acompañado por submarinistas experimentados. En nuestro país existen muchos clubs de submarinismo en los que podrás realizar el curso de iniciación. En la Federación de tu Comunidad Autónoma te facilitarán un listado con los centros más próximos a tu domicilio.

- **Inicio:** todo el año.
- **Duración:** 2-3 semanas.
- **Horario:** de lunes a viernes tardes-noche, fines de semana.
- **Grupos:** 5 y 10 personas.
- **Precio:** entre 40.000 y 45.000 ptas.
- **Teléfonos:**

- Federació Catalana d'Activitats Subaquàtiques. Tel. (93) 330 44 72.
- Federación Andaluza de Actividades Subacuáticas.Tel. (950) 27 06 12.
- Federación Madrileña de Actividades Subacuáticas. Tel. (91) 442 21 69.
- Federación Balear de Actividades Subacuáticas. Tel. (971) 46 33 15.
- Federación Española de Actividades Subacuáticas. Tel. (93) 200 67 69.

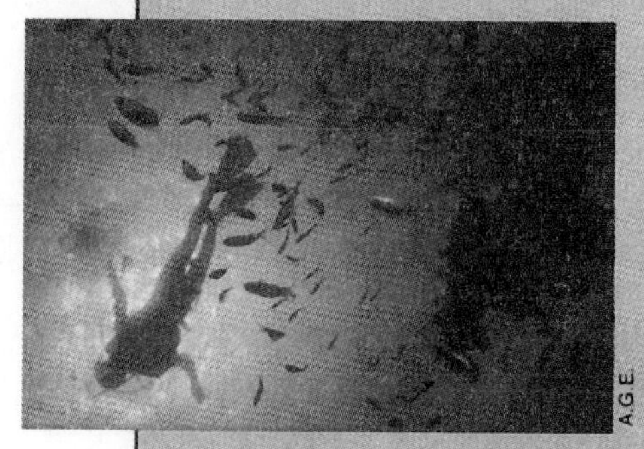

La Federación de Actividades Subacuáticas de tu Comunidad te informará de dónde puedes aprender.

te atrae... *you are attracted by . . .*
iniciación *introduction*
buceador *diver*
titulación *qualification, license*
te permitirá bucear *it will allow you to dive*

Nombre ______________________ Fecha ____________

W7-11 Conteste las preguntas con información del artículo.

1. ¿Qué características son necesarias para hacer submarinismo?

   ____

2. ¿Cuánto tiempo dura el curso de iniciación?

   ____

3. Al final del curso, ¿qué titulación va a tener?

   ____

4. ¿Qué le va a permitir esa licencia?

   ____

5. ¿Dónde puede aprender a hacer submarinismo en su comunidad/universidad/escuela?

   ____

Después de leer

W7-12 Diseñe un anuncio de un pasatiempo. En su universidad o en su comunidad enseñan a nadar, a patinar, a navegar o a esquiar. Escriba un anuncio de esta actividad para su universidad o su comunidad, en español para la comunidad hispana.

Ejemplo: *¿Quiere aprender a navegar para el verano? El centro de la comunidad de Mystic tiene clases de navegación los meses de junio y julio. Las clases son todos los sábados de las ocho de la mañana hasta las doce del día.*

____

____

____

____

____

W7-13 Hablen sobre sus diseños en la clase y expliquen lo que pueden aprender en las diferentes comunidades.

¡A escribir!

Antes de escribir

W7-14 Haga una lista de sus pasatiempos favoritos durante las siguientes estaciones del año.

Primavera	Verano	Otoño	Invierno
________	________	________	________
________	________	________	________
________	________	________	________
________	________	________	________

Nombre ______________________________ Fecha ________________

Phrases: greeting; inviting, accepting, and declining; saying good-bye; stating a preference; writing a letter (informal)
Vocabulary: leisure; sports; time expressions
Grammar: verbs: present, irregular preterite, preterite

Vamos a escribir

W7-15 Usted va a escribirle una carta a Alicia Benson o a otra persona que sabe de sus pasatiempos y deportes favoritos.

1. Begin by asking how he/she is. 2. Next, ask if he/she has something to do tonight, if he/she likes sports, and if so, which sport he/she practices and when. What other activities does he/she like and not like, and what is one thing he/she never does on Saturdays? 3. End by asking him/her if he/she would like to do something with you next week.

____
(la fecha de hoy)

*Querido(a)*________________________

*Tu amigo(a)*________________________

Nombre ______________________ Fecha ______________

Después de escribir

W7-16 Ahora imagínese que usted es Alicia o la persona que recibió la carta. Conteste la carta que recibió.

____
(la fecha de hoy)

Querido(a) ______________

____

____

____

____

____

____

____

____

____

____

____

____

____

____

____

____

____

Tu amigo(a) ______________

Actividades y ejercicios orales

PRONUNCIACIÓN ESENCIAL

Spanish *c* and *z*

CD2-2 **W7-17** In Latin America and some areas in Spain, **z** and the letter **c** before **e** or **i** are pronounced like the *s* in *swim*. Listen to the following sentences and repeat after the speaker.

—¡Martín! ¡Pancho! Es hora de almor**z**ar.
—No podemos, mamá. Vamos a ha**c**er ejer**c**i**c**io.
—Y qué van a ha**c**er que es tan importante?
—Vamos al parque a montar en bi**c**icleta. ¿Podemos llevarnos el almuer**z**o?
—¡Ay, cómo no!... ¿Qué voy a ha**c**er con ellos?

CD2-3 **W7-18** In most of Spain, **z** and **c** before **e** or **i** are pronounced like the *th* in *think*. Listen to the following sentences and repeat after the speaker.

—Vi**c**ente, ¿quieres ir al con**c**ierto de "A**z**úcar Moreno" en Bar**c**elona?
—Sí, **C**e**c**ilia. Me gustaría ir. Me gusta su música.
—El con**c**ierto es el quin**c**e de mar**z**o. Comien**z**a a las **c**inco de la tarde.
—Quieres **c**enar después del con**c**ierto? Cono**z**co unos restaurantes fabulosos.
—Vale.

CD2-4 **W7-19** In all other positions, Spanish **c** has a hard sound like the *c* in *car*. Listen to the following sentences and repeat after the speaker.

—Voy a ir al parque a **c**aminar, Silvia. ¿Me a**c**ompañas?
—Sí, **c**ómo no, Jaime. Pero hace mucho **c**alor.
—Después de la **c**aminata, te invito a tomar una **C**o**c**a-**C**ola.
—Qué simpáti**c**o eres, Jaime!

Spanish *q*

CD2-5 **W7-20** Spanish **q** also has a hard *k* sound as in *Katy*. In written form, **q** is always followed by **u**. Listen to the following sentences and repeat after the speaker.

—Silvia, ¿**q**uieres ir a **Q**uito a visitar a mis padres este fin de semana?
—Es una buena idea, **q**uerido. ¿No es el cumpleaños de tu papá?
—Sí, es el **q**uince de este mes.
—¿**Q**ué le llevamos de regalo?
—Bueno... a él le gusta el e**q**uipo nacional de fútbol. ¿**Q**ué tal dos billetes para un partido?
—¡Perfecto!

Nombre ______________________________ Fecha ______________

EN CONTEXTO

CD2-6 **W7-21 ¡Vamos a la playa!** Escuche la siguiente conversación. Decida si las siguientes oraciones son verdaderas **(V)**, falsas **(F)** o si no hay suficiente información **(N)** para contestar.

1. _____ David visita a Alicia en México.
2. _____ El trabajo de Alicia fue muy interesante.
3. _____ Alicia fue a un partido de fútbol entre México y Chile.
4. _____ Ellos van a nadar en el mar.
5. _____ David está contento de ver a Alicia.

VOCABULARIO ESENCIAL

CD2-7 **W7-22 Pasatiempos en Santiago de Chile.** Escuche la descripción de los pasatiempos de David y Alicia en Santiago. Escriba los números del 1 al 5 en el orden en que las actividades se describen.

_____ a. Compraron boletos para ir a ver un partido de fútbol.

_____ b. Caminaron por el Parque de la República.

_____ c. Tomaron fotografías del Palacio de Bellas Artes.

_____ d. Fueron al viñedo.

_____ e. Fueron a las tiendas de compras.

CD2-8 **W7-23 Mi experiencia en Monterrey.** Alicia le está contando sus experiencias a David en México. Complete las oraciones a continuación para completar las ideas de Alicia.

1. Mi familia fue ______________________________.
2. Con los amigos fuimos a ______________________________.
3. Una noche oímos cantar ______________________________.
4. Los Mariachis cantaron ______________________________.

CD2-9 **W7-24 Una familia activa.** Todos los meses Alicia llama por teléfono a su mamá. Escuche su conversación y anote qué actividades hizo cada persona el mes pasado. Escriba los nombres de la familia y de los amigos de Alicia donde corresponda.

Persona(s)	**Actividad**
1. ______________________	Jugó al fútbol.
2. ______________________	Fue a la Florida.
3. ______________________	Compró un libro sobre vinos chilenos.
4. ______________________	Tomó clases de golf.
5. ______________________	Corrió y ganó un maratón.
6. ______________________	Llamó para saber de ti.
7. ______________________	Comenzó a hacer ejercicio.

Nombre ______________________ Fecha ____________

LECCIÓN 8 ¡SALUD Y BUEN PROVECHO!

Cuaderno de ejercicios

VOCABULARIO ESENCIAL

W8-1 **¿Qué comen estas personas?** Mire los siguientes dibujos y complete las oraciones con las comidas y bebidas apropiadas.

1. David come ______________________

____

____

____

y toma/bebe ______________________

____

2. Alicia come ______________________

____

____

____

y toma/bebe ______________________

____

3. La señora Torreón come ______________________

____

____

____

y toma/bebe ______________________

____

4. El señor Torreón come ______________________

____

____

____

y toma/bebe ______________________

____

Nombre ______________________ Fecha ______________

W8-2 ¡Planifique el menú! Usted va a ayudar a la señora Torreón a planificar un menú para esta noche. Piense en una entrada, un plato principal, un vegetal, un postre y bebidas. Escriba las comidas que usted quiere incluir en el menú a continuación.

de entrada:

____

de plato principal:

____

los vegetales:

____

de postre:

____

de bebidas:

____

GRAMÁTICA ESENCIAL

W8-3 En el restaurante. Usted está en un restaurante con unos amigos. Sus amigos le hacen preguntas. Siga el modelo y haga las siguientes cosas: 1. conteste las preguntas de sus amigos con una oración completa; 2. haga un círculo alrededor del objeto directo; 3. escriba la oración otra vez, esta vez con el pronombre correcto **(lo, los, la, las).** Si hay dos posibilidades para la nueva oración, escriba dos oraciones en el espacio indicado.

Ejemplo: ¿Quieres pedir aperativos?

—Sí, quiero pedir aperitivos.

—Sí, quiero pedirlos. No, no los quiero pedir.

1. ¿Estás leyendo la lista de postres?

____

____

____

2. ¿Tomas el café con azúcar o sin azúcar?

____

____

____

3. ¿Pediste las papas fritas?

____

____

____

4. ¿Conoces los restaurantes de la ciudad de Chile?

____

____

____

5. ¿Vas a pedir los mariscos esta noche?

____

____

____

6. ¿Bebes vino tinto?

____

____

____

7. ¿Vas a pagar la cuenta?

____

____

____

W8-4 En la cocina. Los señores Torreón están conversando en su cocina. Lea su conversación y llene los espacios indicados con la forma correcta de pronombre de objeto directo apropiado **(lo, la, los, las).**

Rodolfo: ¿Ya preparaste el desayuno, Rosario?

Rosario: Sí, Rodolfo, ya __________ preparé. Aquí tienes tu café con leche y tu pan tostado.

Rodolfo: ¿Y la mermelada? ¿__________ tienes?

Rosario: Ya no hay mermelada, solamente mantequilla. ¿__________ quieres?

Rodolfo: Sí, gracias. Y por ser domingo, ¿puedo comer huevos fritos? Los huevos fritos, ¿ya __________ preparaste?

Rosario: Sí, y las papas fritas también. ¿__________ quieres probar?

Rodolfo: ¡Cómo no! Ay, Rosario, ¡David tiene razón! Cocinas excelentemente. Gracias, mi amor.

W8-5 Los gustos de los señores Torreón. Los señores Torreón van a un restaurante a almorzar. Hablan sobre la comida que se sirve allí. Lea la conversación en la próxima página y llene los espacios en blanco con las siguientes formas: **lo, la, los** o **las.**

Remember that the direct object pronouns ***(me, te, lo, la, nos, los, las)*** *always answer the question "who(m)?" or "what?"*

Señora Torreón: ¿Con qué quieres almorzar, Rodolfo?

Señor Torreón: Quiero comer carne.

Señora Torreón: ¿__________ quieres comer con papas o con arroz?

Señor Torreón: Quiero comer __________ con papas. Y tú, Rosario, ¿con qué quieres almorzar?

Señora Torreón: Quiero comer pescado al horno.

Señor Torreón: ¿__________ quieres con papas?

Señora Torreón: Sí, exactamente. __________ quiero con papas también. ¿Llamamos al camarero?

Señor Torreón: Señor, por favor, estamos listos para pedir.

Camarero: ¿Con qué desean almorzar los señores?

Señora Torreón: Yo quiero el pescado con papas.

Camarero: Se __________ traigo enseguida. Y usted, señor, ¿qué quiere comer?

Señor Torreón: Yo quiero la carne con papas también.

Camarero: Se __________ traigo enseguida. Y para beber, ¿qué desean?

Señora Torreón: Yo quiero agua mineral.

Camarero: __________ ordeno rápidamente.

Señor Torreón: Yo quiero una copa de vino blanco.

Camarero: Se __________ traigo inmediatamente.

Señora Torreón: Yo quiero un flan de caramelo.

Señor Torreón: Yo también.

Camarero: Se __________ traigo después de la comida. ¿Dos cafés?

Señora Torreón: Sí, nos __________ trae al final con la cuenta. Gracias.

W8-6 Alicia recuerda Monterrey. A continuación Alicia describe cómo era su vida cuando vivía en Monterrey. Ayúdela a completar la historia, poniendo los verbos entre paréntesis en el imperfecto del indicativo.

Cuando yo ______________ (vivir) en Monterrey, ______________ (estar) muy contenta. Yo ______________ (tener) muchas responsibilidades y ______________ (estudiar) constantemente, pero mis amigos y yo ______________ (salir) de vez en cuando, y mis compañeros de clase me ______________ (tratar) muy bien.

En un día típico, yo ______________ (levantarse) a las siete. Mi familia y yo ______________ (desayunar) con pan y café, y después yo ______________ (caminar) a mis clases. Por la tarde, siempre ______________ (tomar) un café con algún amigo. Por la noche, nosotros ______________ (comer) en casa, y nosotros todos ______________ (acostarse) para las once. ¡Qué vida tan linda!

Nombre ______________________ Fecha __________

Cultura

W8-7 Por el mundo hispano. Lea las siguientes oraciones y decida si son verdaderas **(V)** o falsas **(F).** Si una oración es falsa, corríjala para que sea verdadera.

1. _____ La comida corriente es la comida a precio fijo.
2. _____ En muchos restaurantes españoles y latinoamericanos hay una sección de no fumar.
3. _____ El camarero no trae la cuenta hasta que usted se la pida.
4. _____ La cuenta siempre incluye la propina.
5. _____ En general, el desayuno consiste en una taza de café, pan con mermelada o mantequilla y, a veces, fruta.
6. _____ La sobremesa es la costumbre de dormir la siesta después del almuerzo.
7. _____ Se sirve la cena más tarde que en los Estados Unidos. Generalmente es después de las siete de la noche.
8. _____ Algunos hispanos comen una merienda entre las cinco y las seis de la tarde.
9. _____ La tortilla de maíz es una tapa muy común que se sirve con jamón y queso.
10. _____ En los bares de tapas se sirven solamente bebidas alcohólicas como vino y cerveza.

¡A leer!: El restaurante Versailles

Antes de leer

W8-8

1. Típicamente, ¿qué información se incluye en el menú de un restaurante?

____

____

____

____

2. ¿Cómo se organiza la información en un menú normalmente?

____

____

____

____

3. ¿Qué parte del menú mira Ud. primero cuando va a un restaurante?

____

____

____

____

Nombre ______________________________ Fecha ______________

Vamos a leer

W8-9 Mire el menú a continuación y busque esa información.

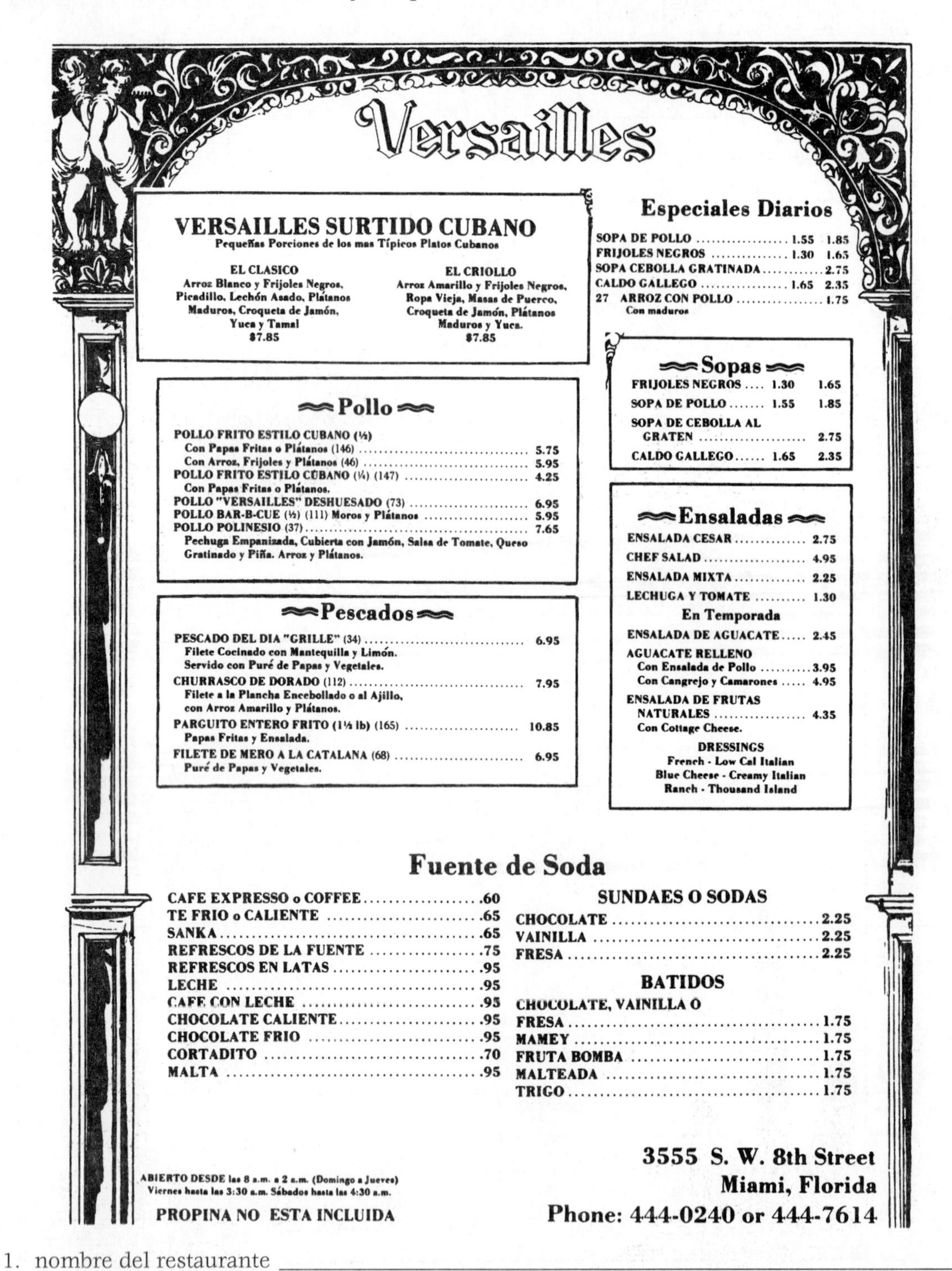

Versailles

VERSAILLES SURTIDO CUBANO

Pequeñas Porciones de los mas Típicos Platos Cubanos

EL CLASICO
Arroz Blanco y Frijoles Negros, Picadillo, Lechón Asado, Plátanos Maduros, Croqueta de Jamón, Yuca y Tamal
$7.85

EL CRIOLLO
Arroz Amarillo y Frijoles Negros, Ropa Vieja, Masas de Puerco, Croqueta de Jamón, Plátanos Maduros y Yuca.
$7.85

Especiales Diarios

SOPA DE POLLO	1.55	1.85
FRIJOLES NEGROS	1.30	1.65
SOPA CEBOLLA GRATINADA		2.75
CALDO GALLEGO	1.65	2.35
27 ARROZ CON POLLO Con maduros		1.75

Pollo

POLLO FRITO ESTILO CUBANO (½)	
Con Papas Fritas o Plátanos (146)	5.75
Con Arroz, Frijoles y Plátanos (46)	5.95
POLLO FRITO ESTILO CUBANO (¼) (147) Con Papas Fritas o Plátanos.	4.25
POLLO "VERSAILLES" DESHUESADO (73)	6.95
POLLO BAR-B-CUE (½) (111) Moros y Plátanos	5.95
POLLO POLINESIO (37) Pechuga Empanizada, Cubierta con Jamón, Salsa de Tomate, Queso Gratinado y Piña. Arroz y Plátanos.	7.65

Sopas

FRIJOLES NEGROS	1.30	1.65
SOPA DE POLLO	1.55	1.85
SOPA DE CEBOLLA AL GRATEN		2.75
CALDO GALLEGO	1.65	2.35

Pescados

PESCADO DEL DIA "GRILLE" (34) Filete Cocinado con Mantequilla y Limón. Servido con Puré de Papas y Vegetales.	6.95
CHURRASCO DE DORADO (112) Filete a la Plancha Encebollado o al Ajillo, con Arroz Amarillo y Plátanos.	7.95
PARGUITO ENTERO FRITO (1½ lb) (165) Papas Fritas y Ensalada.	10.85
FILETE DE MERO A LA CATALANA (68) Puré de Papas y Vegetales.	6.95

Ensaladas

ENSALADA CESAR	2.75
CHEF SALAD	4.95
ENSALADA MIXTA	2.25
LECHUGA Y TOMATE	1.30
En Temporada	
ENSALADA DE AGUACATE	2.45
AGUACATE RELLENO	
Con Ensalada de Pollo	3.95
Con Cangrejo y Camarones	4.95
ENSALADA DE FRUTAS NATURALES Con Cottage Cheese.	4.35

DRESSINGS
French - Low Cal Italian
Blue Cheese - Creamy Italian
Ranch - Thousand Island

Fuente de Soda

CAFE EXPRESSO o COFFEE	.60
TE FRIO o CALIENTE	.65
SANKA	.65
REFRESCOS DE LA FUENTE	.75
REFRESCOS EN LATAS	.95
LECHE	.95
CAFE CON LECHE	.95
CHOCOLATE CALIENTE	.95
CHOCOLATE FRIO	.95
CORTADITO	.70
MALTA	.95

SUNDAES O SODAS

CHOCOLATE	2.25
VAINILLA	2.25
FRESA	2.25

BATIDOS

CHOCOLATE, VAINILLA O FRESA	1.75
MAMEY	1.75
FRUTA BOMBA	1.75
MALTEADA	1.75
TRIGO	1.75

ABIERTO DESDE las 8 a.m. a 2 a.m. (Domingo a Jueves)
Viernes hasta las 3:30 a.m. Sábados hasta las 4:30 a.m.

PROPINA NO ESTA INCLUIDA

3555 S. W. 8th Street
Miami, Florida
Phone: 444-0240 or 444-7614

1. nombre del restaurante ______________________________
2. dirección ______________________________
3. ciudad ______________________________
4. cuándo está abierto *(open)* ______________________________

Nombre ______________________________ Fecha ______________

W8-10 Haga un círculo alrededor de todas las palabras que usted reconoce en el menú.

W8-11 Escriba las categorías principales que usted encuentra en el menú y una comida o bebida de cada categoría que a usted le gusta.

Categoría

1. ______________________
2. ______________________
3. ______________________

Comida o bebida

1. ______________________
2. ______________________
3. ______________________

W8-12 ¿Qué tipo de restaurante es el Versailles? Escriba el nombre de un plato típico que se sirve allí.

____

Después de leer

W8-13 Imagínese que usted fue a cenar al Restaurante Versailles. Escríbale una carta al (a la) dueño(a) del restaurante y dígale si le gustó la comida y por qué, o si no le gustó, explíquele por qué no.

Nombre ______________________ Fecha ____________

¡A escribir!

Antes de escribir

W8-14 Lea cada descripción e identifique si es carne, postre, bebida, fruta o verdura. Luego identifique qué es.

Ejemplo: Cuando hace calor, se toma frío en un vaso grande, pero contiene cafeína. Se le puede poner limón.
bebida, té

1. Se pone en el cereal y se bebe también. Se le puede poner chocolate.
____
2. Es uno de los ingredientes principales de una ensalada básica y es de color rojo.
____
3. Es frío y viene en sabores de fruta, chocolate o vainilla y contiene muchas calorías.
____
4. Viene de un animal que pone huevos *(lays eggs)* y es la parte principal de una comida.
____
5. Se come con un bistec de varias maneras: frita, asada con mantequilla, etcétera.
____

W8-15 ¿Cuáles son sus comidas y bebidas preferidas en casa y en los restaurantes? Escriba sus respuestas con oraciones completas.

En casa

1. ¿Con qué desayuna usted normalmente?
____
____
2. ¿Qué toma usted para el desayuno?
____
____
3. ¿Con qué almuerza generalmente?
____
____
4. ¿Come usted merienda entre *(between)* comidas? ¿Qué come?
____
____
5. ¿Con qué le gusta cenar?
____
____

6. ¿Qué comidas étnicas sabe usted preparar?

7. ¿Cuál es su postre preferido?

8. ¿Qué comidas fritas come usted?

9. ¿Qué carne prefiere usted?

10. ¿Qué toma usted cuando tiene mucha sed?

En el restaurante

1. ¿Qué comida le gusta pedir cuando va a un restaurante?

2. ¿Qué comidas de otros países le gusta pedir en un restaurante? ¿De qué países son?

3. ¿Qué restaurantes étnicos hay en su ciudad?

4. ¿Cuál es su restaurante preferido?

5. ¿Qué bebidas pide usted con más frecuencia en un restaurante?

6. ¿Cuándo le gusta ir a los restaurantes?

Phrases: appreciating food; asking the price

Vocabulary: food: bread, cereals, drinks, fish & seafood, fruits, legumes & vegetables, meals, meat; restaurant

Vamos a escribir

W8-16 Usted es dueño(a) ***(owner)*** **de un restaurante.** ¿Qué tipo de restaurante es? ¿Cómo se llama? ¿Qué comida sirve usted en su restaurante? ¿Qué bebidas hay? Diseñe *(Design)* un menú a continuación. Incluya el nombre del restaurante, su dirección, su número de teléfono, las comidas y bebidas que usted va a ofrecer y los precios.

Nombre ______________________ Fecha ____________

Después de escribir

W8-17 Los señores Torreón almorzaron en su restaurante preferido esta tarde. Prepare su cuenta abajo. En la cuenta no se olvide de incluir el nombre de su restaurante, la dirección y el número de teléfono.

Nombre ______________________ Fecha ______________

Cultura

W8-18 Lectura. Lea las siguientes preguntas primero. Luego lea la historia sobre el origen del helado en la página siguiente y conteste las preguntas.

1. Lea el título del artículo. ¿De qué se trata?

 ____

2. Según el primer párrafo de la lectura, ¿dónde y cuándo nació el helado?

 ____

3. ¿Quiénes dieron a conocer *(made known)* el uso del helado en el siglo XVII?

 ____

4. ¿En qué partes geográficas lo dieron a conocer?

 ____

5. ¿Cuándo se introdujo el helado al continente americano? ______________ en los Estados Unidos y ______________.

6. La "nieve" se preparaba con ______________, ______________ y ______________.

7. ¿Cómo se llama y dónde está la primera heladería que ofreció el helado? ¿En qué ciudad está?

 ____

8. ¿Cómo se llama la persona que introdujo el helado a Francia a través de sus cocineros *(chefs, cooks)*?

 ____

9. ¿Qué grupo de emigrantes se dedicó a la producción de leche? ¿Dónde?

 ____

10. ¿Qué es la "Flor de Leche" europea?

 ____

11. ¿Por qué se considera el helado de Danesa uno de los diez mejores helados del continente?

 ____

Nombre ______________________________ Fecha ______________

La aparición de los helados data de hace 600 años aproximadamente. Se cree que fue en Italia donde nació el tipo de helado que actualmente conocemos, aunque en ese entonces su elaboración era solamente doméstica.

Fueron también los italianos —genoveses y venecianos— del siglo XVII, quienes lo dieron a conocer, dado los nexos comerciales que tenían con las distintas regiones de Asia y norte de Europa, posteriormente, éstos últimos, propagaron las recetas en sus países antes del descubrimiento de América.

En el continente Americano, el helado se introdujo durante la colonización de los ingleses, hace más de 200 años en Estados Unidos de Norteamérica y en México, apenas unos 40 años.

Cabe señalar que en nuestro país durante la época porfiriana ya existía una forma de helado, mejor conocida como "nieve", la cual era preparada con agua, fruta y azúcar. Era algo derivado del raspado, que conocieron aquí los españoles en el Imperio de Moctezuma II. El raspado, era un tipo de golosina helada que consistía en hielo picado al que se le agregaba una miel de frutas como el capulín, garambuyo, tuna o tejocote, posteriormente, naranja y limón.

Fue en Francia, donde por primera vez, el helado se elaboró con fines comerciales, siendo el Café Precope, la primera heladería ofrecida al público consumidor y la cual aún existe en París. Se cuenta que Catalina de Medici introdujo esta golosina a través de sus cocineros.

En nuestro continente, debido a la escasa relación —casi nula— entre los sajones americanos y los latinoamericanos, el conocimiento del helado de crema fue muy tardío. Este ocurrió después de la independencia de las colonias americanas, pues antes los intereses religiosos y costumbristas de los europeos, impedían todo tipo de comunicación o intercambio ideológico entre los pobladores.

Por otra parte, tocó a México el privilegio de ser el primer país latinoamericano en conocer el helado de crema, gracias a la afluencia de emigrantes de origen europeo que se dedicaron a la producción de leche, desarrollando una infraestructura adecuada para su impulso comercial.

Este gran empuje, se dio principalmente en la región del Bajío, donde el terreno era propio para la producción lechera, a diferencia de las cuencas poblana, queretana y mexiquense. Así, se vio nacer por primera vez un helado con todas las características cualitativas y naturales, superiores a la "Flor de Leche" europea, nombre original del helado de crema.

En México, aunque ya se tenía conocimiento de este tipo de helado, fue Industrias *Danesa*, quien en golpe de iniciativa se arriesgo a presentar ante el público consumidor un auténtico helado, el cual, primero por curiosidad o por novedad, empezó a tener aceptación hasta hacerse un hábito alimenticio en la dieta mexicana.

Actualmente, el helado de Danesa, está ubicado entres los diez mejores helados del continente, dada la calidad de sus ingredientes y el tipo de leche que se produce en la cuenca del Bajío.

Actividades y ejercicios orales

PRONUNCIACIÓN ESENCIAL

Spanish *ll* and *y*

CD2-10 **W8-19** Pronunciation of **ll** and **y** varies widely in the Spanish-speaking world. In general, **ll** and initial **y** are pronounced like the *y* in *yo-yo*. As you know, the word **y** *(and)* is pronounced like the *i* in *machine*. Listen to the following sentences and repeat after the speaker.

—Alicia, te presento a mi amiga **Y**olanda **Y**añez de Cari**ll**o. E**ll**a es de Sevi**ll**a.
—Mucho gusto, **Y**olanda. ¿Cuándo **ll**egaste a Chile?
—**Ll**egué a las dos de la tarde a**y**er y **ll**amé a Rosario inmediatamente.
—¿Quieres desa**y**unar con nosotros mañana? Vamos a desa**y**unar en la terraza del hotel si no **ll**ueve.
—Sí, gracias.

Spanish *ñ*

CD2-11 **W8-20** Spanish **ñ** is pronounced approximately like the *ny* sound in *canyon*. Listen to the following sentences and repeat after the speaker.

—¿Dónde están los ni**ñ**os, Alicia?
—Creo que Miguel está ba**ñ**ándose y Shawn está jugando al fútbol con su compa**ñ**ero de escuela. Oye, mañana es el cumpleaños de Shawn, ¿verdad?
—No, Alicia. Ma**ñ**ana es mi cumplea**ñ**os.
—Ay, ¿sí? ¡Feliz cumplea**ñ**os, I**ñ**aki!
—Gracias.

EN CONTEXTO

CD2-12 **W8-21** **¡Salud!** Escuche la siguiente conversación. Decida si las siguientes oraciones son verdaderas **(V)**, falsas **(F)** o si no hay suficiente información **(N)** para contestar.

1. _____ Los señores Torreón invitaron a Alicia a cenar en su casa.
2. _____ Los señores Torreón son buenos cocineros.
3. _____ David es también un buen cocinero.
4. _____ El guisado es de pollo y papas.
5. _____ La comida huele muy bien.

Nombre ______________________________ Fecha ______________

VOCABULARIO ESENCIAL

CD2-13 **W8-22 ¡Tengo ganas de comer!** David siempre tiene hambre. Ahora está en Viña del Mar con Alicia, después de nadar y de hacer submarinismo. David tiene hambre y le pregunta a Alicia si tiene hambre también. Escuche muy bien la conversación entre David y Alicia y escoja la mejor respuesta para completar cada oración.

1. _____ David tiene...
   a. sed.
   b. hambre.
   c. sueño.

2. _____ Alicia tiene...
   a. hambre.
   b. razón.
   c. sed.

3. _____ David quiere almorzar con ...
   a. carne con papas fritas.
   b. sopa y ensalada.
   c. pescado con arroz.

4. _____ Alicia quiere almorzar...
   a. sopa.
   b. ensalada.
   c. carne con arroz.

5. _____ De postre, David quiere...
   a. arroz con leche.
   b. flan.
   c. helado de vainilla.

CD2-14 **W8-23 Las comidas.** Escuche la siguiente narración de David. Mientras escucha la conversación, haga un círculo alrededor de las comidas que David va a comer hoy. No vamos a usar todos los dibujos.

Nombre ______________________ Fecha __________

LECCIÓN 9 ¿VACACIONES DE VERANO EN DICIEMBRE?

Cuaderno de ejercicios

VOCABULARIO ESENCIAL

W9-1 Asociaciones. Empareje las siguientes palabras con la oración más lógica. No va a tener que usar todas las palabras de la lista.

los aretes	los juegos de video	el reproductor de DVD
el anillo	la máquina de afeitar	la cámara de fotografía digital
la pulsera	la radiograbadora	el escáner plano
el collar	el secador de pelo	el juego de pesas
la computadora	la cámara de video	la caminadora
el reproductor de CD portátil		

1. Se usa para navegar el Internet ______________________
2. Joya que se lleva en la muñeca ______________________
3. Joyas que se llevan en los dedos ______________________
4. Se usa para sacar fotos para ver en la computadora ______________________
5. Se usa para ver películas en disco ______________________
6. Game Cube, Game Station, etcétera ______________________
7. Se usa para tener músculos *(muscles)* muy fuertes ______________________
8. Se usa para secar el pelo ______________________
9. Es para escuchar música mientras se corre en el parque ______________________
10. Joyas que se llevan en las orejas ______________________

GRAMÁTICA ESENCIAL

W9-2 Hermanos opuestos *(opposites)*. Shawn y su amigo Miguel son opuestos. Lo que hace Shawn no lo hace Miguel. Cambie las oraciones siguentes para reflejar las diferencias entre los dos hermanos.

Ejemplo: Shawn siempre le trae rosas a su mamá. (nunca / nada)
Miguel nunca le trae nada a su mamá.

1. Shawn siempre estudia. (nunca)

   Miguel ______________________.

2. A Miguel le gustan todos los deportes. (ningún)

   A Shawn ______________________.

3. Miguel conoce a todos los estudiantes de la escuela. (nadie)

   Shawn ____.

4. Shawn siempre juega al básquetbol y al fútbol con sus amigos. (ni... ni / con nadie)

   Miguel ____.

W9-3 De mal humor *(In a bad mood)*. David está de mal humor hoy con sus amigos. A todos les contesta negativamente. Escriba lo que responde David a las preguntas usando las palabras entre paréntesis.

Ejemplo: ¿Quieres nadar conmigo *(with me)* hoy? (con nadie / nunca)
No, no quiero nadar con nadie nunca.

1. ¿Practicas algún deporte? (ningún)

   ____

2. ¿Te gusta nadar? (tampoco)

   ____

3. ¿Prefieres jugar al tenis? (nunca / con nadie)

   ____

4. ¿Te gusta correr o jugar al básquetol? (ni... ni)

   ____

W9-4 Sí y no. Escriba las siguientes oraciones dos veces: primero, positivamente y después, negativamente.

Ejemplo: David / siempre / levantarse / a tiempo / para / ir / a / trabajar
David siempre se levanta a tiempo para ir a trabajar.
David nunca se levanta a tiempo para ir a trabajar.

1. el señor Torreón / siempre / regalarle / o / flores / o / dulces / a / la señora Torreón

   ____

   ____

2. yo / pensar / visitar / Viña / también

   ____

   ____

3. Alicia, ¿hay / algunos / brazaletes / bonitos / aquí?

   ____

   ____

4. David, ¿tú / ver / algo / barato / en / almacén?

   ____

   ____

Nombre ______________________ Fecha ____________

W9-5 Así era yo. Alicia le describe a los señores Torreón las cosas que ella hacía con su familia en Wisconsin.

Ejemplo: mi familia y yo / ir a esquiar los fines de semana
Mi familia y yo íbamos a esquiar los fines de semana.

1. yo / comer muchos chocolates cuando mi mamá no / estar en casa
____
____
2. mis hermanaos / jugar al fútbol todos los días
____
____
3. mis hermanos y yo / montar en bicicleta todo el tiempo
____
____
4. mi papá / trabajar mucho en casa los fines de semana
____
____
5. mi mamá / hacer comida típica para el día de Navidad
____
____
6. mi familia y yo / ir a Chicago y a los museos en el verano
____
____
7. nosotros / divertirse mucho juntos
____
____

W9-6 Hace muchos años... La señora Torreón describe su vida cuando era joven a Alicia y a David. Complete el siguiente relato usando la forma correcta del imperfecto.

Cuando tenía doce años, ______________ (vivir) en una casa en Viña. Cuando ______________ (tener) dieciocho años, regresamos a Santiago y así asistí a la Universidad de Santiago. En la universidad, me ______________ (gustar) ver los juegos de fútbol y ______________ (practicar) tenis todos los fines de semana durante el verano. En el invierno ______________ (ir) con mi familia a esquiar. Mis amigos y yo ______________ (ir) a patinar los viernes por la noche. Después de patinar, ______________ (cenar) en casa de alguna de las muchachas y después ______________ (cantar) y ______________ (bailar) toda la noche. Nosotros lo ______________ (pasar) muy bien en la universidad. Ahora administro este viñedo y recuerdo mi vida de joven con ustedes.

Nombre ______________________________ Fecha ____________

Cultura

W9-7 La religión en Hispanoamérica. Lea cada oración y decida si es verdadera **(V)**, falsa **(F)** o si no hay información suficiente **(N)** para contestar.

1. _____ Los españoles trajeron a América la religión católica.
2. _____ Los indígenas no tenían religión cuando llegaron los españoles.
3. _____ Hoy en día, los santos tienen mucha importancia en Latinoamérica.
4. _____ La religión que llegó de África influyó en un 80% en la religión de Latinoamérica.

W9-8 Celebraciones. Complete las siguientes oraciones sobre las celebraciones en el mundo hispano.

1. En España, comienza la celebración de la Navidad ______________________.
2. En España y en Puerto Rico, los niños reciben sus regalos el día de ______________.
3. En México, las posadas ______________________________________.
4. En Venezuela, la gente patina después de ______________________.

W9-9 Lectura. Lea las siguientes cartas a Santa Claus y llene el cuadro de la página siguiente con la información que usted encuentra en las cartas.

Cartitas a Santa Claus

"Querido Santa: Yo quiero un juego Super Nintendo, un auto de radio control y un teléfono celular para llamar a mis amiguitos." (Danielito, 7 años, Santa Ana)

"Querido Santa: Quisiera una muñeca nueva, porque Peggy se fue con otro." (Gustavo, 20 años, Orange)

"Querido Santa Claus: Lo único que yo quisiera es un auto nuevo y grande, para mi esposo Raúl, así yo puedo pasear con los niños e ir al supermercado todos los días y prestárselo de vez en cuando." (Carmen, 30 años, Costa Mesa)

"Queridísimo Santa: Sólo te pido un marido con mucho, mucho dinero. No te pido que sea joven, ni guapo ni simpático para no parecer demasiado presuntuosa." (Claudia, 19 años, Irvine)

"Mi viejo y querido Santa Claus: No te pido nada para mí. Sólo quisiera ganar el Lotto para mi cuenta bancaria." (Reynaldo, 40 años, Mission Viejo)

"Santa: Yo sé que para esta época del año todo el mundo te escribe pidiendo cosas. Yo, en cambio, te escribo para ofrecerte algo. Ahí, en el frente de mi casa, tengo una cochera vacía. ¿No quisieras dejar estacionado tu BMW hasta la próxima Navidad que yo te lo cuido? (No te olvides de dejarme las llaves en el buzón." (Alejandro, 19 años, Buena Park)

"Querido Santa: ¿Podrías traerme un televisor que pase algo de deportes? Porque en mi casa, entre mi esposa y mis tres hijas, todos los televisores sólo pasan telenovelas..." (Julián, 50 años, Garden Grove)

"Querido Santa: Yo quiero un hermanito, pero de esos que no lloran ni usan mis juguetes y que pueda jugar conmigo a las luchas y me pueda ayudar en las tareas de la escuela. (Gabrielito, 6 años, Anaheim)

"Kerido Zanta: Me ase falta un dixionario. Grasiaz." (Eduardo, 12 años, Huntington Beach)

"Querido Santa: Soy alegre, tengo buena figura y buen carácter. Quisiera que me mandes un novio moreno, de ojos grandes y mucho pelo en el pecho." (El Mariposón Rebelde, 22 años, Newport Beach)

"Querido Santa: Mi hermanito Roberto dice que tú no existes y que los regalos los compra nuestro papá. Yo sé que todo eso es mentira y que tú sí existes. Por eso te pido que me traigas una linda muñeca, de esas que caminan, y te lleves a Roberto que lo único que hace es molestar." (Lupita, 7 años, Fullerton)

Nombre ______________________ Fecha ______________

Persona	Edad	Los regalos que quiere	¿Por qué los quiere?
Danielito	*7 años*	*Super Nintendo, auto de radio control, teléfono celular*	*para llamar a sus amigos*
Carmen		*un auto nuevo y grande*	
	19 años	*un marido*	
		ganar el Lotto	*para su cuenta bancaria*
Gabrielito	*6 años*		
Eduardo			*porque lo necesita*
	7 años	*una muñeca en vez de Roberto*	

¡A leer!: La historia de la tarjeta de Navidad

Antes de leer

W9-10 La siguiente lectura es sobre la historia de la tarjeta de Navidad. Haga una lista con la información que usted espera encontrar en esta lectura.

____

____

____

____

____

Vamos a leer

HISTORIA

La costumbre de mandar tarjetas de Navidad, tal como las conocemos, comenzó en Londres en 1848.

La idea fue de un próspero comerciante, quien le pidió al artista John Calcott Horsley, de la Real Academia, que le diseñara algo para mandar a sus amigos y relacionados saludándolos por Navidad.

La tarjeta estaba dividida en tres paneles, con la ilustración principal mostrando a una familia brindando en una fiesta. Los paneles de ambos lados ilustraban dos antiguas tradiciones de Navidad — dando de comer a los pobres y vistiendo a los necesitados. Un breve mensaje, deseando una alegre Navidad y un feliz año nuevo, acompañaba la ilustración.

En Inglaterra, las tarjetas se comenzaron a imprimir y popularizar en los años que siguieron. Como salieron tres años después que se había pasado en Inglaterra una ley que permitía el envío de cartas por un centavo, las tarjetas fueron recibidas con entusiasmo.

Durante las primeras décadas, las tarjetas más populares eran las de paisajes, niños, flores, pájaros y animales. También se vendían escenas religiosas.

Para 1870, en Boston, se había perfeccionado el proceso de impresión en colores y las reproducciones eran tan bien hechas que sólo los expertos podían distinguir entre una impresión y un original.

Para 1881 la editorial de Boston imprimía 5 millones de tarjetas al año, la mayoría de Navidad.

A comienzos de siglo, las postales alemanas de a centavo invadieron el mercado. La compañía de Boston no podía competir sin bajar la calidad y cerró. Alemania monopolizó el mercado hasta la I Guerra Mundial.

La mayoría de los impresores de tarjetas de saludo surgieron en 1910 y para 1920 ya ofrecían una variedad de diseños y mensajes.

Fue en 1929, cuando la Depresión golpeó al país, que las tarjetas expresando fe y esperanza para mejores tiempos se popularizaron.

La industria sobrevivió la Depresión y para la II Guerra los mensajes reflejaban los sentimientos de la época, apareciendo saludos a través de las millas o expresando añoranza.

Durante unos años se vendían mucho las tarjetas con versos cómicos. Amoldándose a los tiempos, aparecieron los mensajes de paz y los diseños celebrando la llegada del hombre a la Luna. Luego siguieron las tarjetas que reflejaban el afán de mantenerse en buena salud. Hasta a Santa le pusieron patines.

Ahora las valijas del correo se llenan diariamente con millones de artísticos mensajes impresos —sentimentales, picarescos y tradicionales— cada uno es portador de deseos para un cumpleaños, una fiesta u otra ocasión especial. Los modernos diseños y las nuevas técnicas de imprenta hacen que haya tarjetas de todo tipo, tamaño y precio para todas las ocasiones y parentescos.

NACIMIENTO DE UN GIGANTE

Uno de los arquitectos de esta costumbre es el fundador de la compañía de tarjetas Hallmark, Joyce C. Hall, quien se abrigó en una ola de moda de mandar postales y la transformó en una costumbre social que no da indicios de estar por desaparecer.

El negocio comenzó en 1910 y desde entonces se ha convertido en una corporación millonaria y en líder de su industria.

Hallmark es ahora una organización internacional con sede en Kansas City, estado de Missouri, publica más de 11 millones de tarjetas cada día, las imprime en 20 idiomas y las distribuye en más de 100 países.

W9-11 Complete la historia de la tarjeta de Navidad.

Según *(According to)* la historia de mandar tarjetas de Navidad, la costumbre comenzó en el año ______________ en ______________. Fue idea de un ______________ próspero *(prosperous)* quien le pidió al ______________ John Calcott Horsley que diseñara *(he ask . . . to design)* algo especial para mandarles a sus ______________ y ______________ saludándolos *(greeting them)* por ______________.

Nombre ______________________________ Fecha ______________

W9-12 Describa la primera tarjeta. Marque **sí** en todas las descripciones que aplican *(apply)*.

1. ____ Estaba dividida en tres paneles.
2. ____ Estaba dividida en dos ilustraciones principales.
3. ____ La ilustración principal era una familia en una fiesta.
4. ____ Una ilustración era de Santa Claus.
5. ____ Un panel ilustraba tradiciones antiguas *(old)* de Navidad.
6. ____ Un panel ilustraba alguien que daba de comer a *(giving food to)* personas necesitadas *(needy)*.
7. ____ Tenía un breve mensaje *(message)* de un alegre Navidad y un feliz año Nuevo.

W9-13 Qué pasó en los años siguientes? Escriba la letra de la respuesta correcta en el espacio indicado.

a. en 1870
b. en 1881
c. en 1910
d. en 1920
e. en 1929

1. ____ Las tarjetas de la Depresión expresaban la esperanza *(hope)* de mejores tiempos *(better times)*.
2. ____ Se perfeccionó el proceso de impresión en colores *(color printing)* y las reproducciones en las tarjetas.
3. ____ Surgieron la mayoría de impresores *(printers)* de tarjetas de saludo *(greeting cards)*.
4. ____ La editorial de Boston imprimía *(printed)* 5 millones de tarjetas al año.
5. ____ Se ofrecía una variedad de diseños *(designs)* y mensajes.

W9-14 Complete la siguiente oración con los números necesarios.

El negocio de Hallmark, que comenzó en ________________, publica más de ________________ de tarjetas por día y las imprime en ________________ idiomas para distribuirlas en más de ________________ países.

Después de leer

W9-15 Diseñe y dibuje una tarjeta de Navidad, de cumpleaños, de día del santo o de alguna otra ocasión especial para dársela a un(a) compañero(a) de clase. Su diseño puede ser como el de las primeras tarjetas de 1848 o un diseño moderno.

Nombre ______________________________ Fecha ______________

¡A escribir!

Antes de escribir

W9-16 Complete las siguientes oraciones de una manera breva para describir su juventud.

Cuando yo tenía diez años...

1. Mi deporte favorito era ______________________________.
2. Mi día festivo preferido era ______________________________.
3. Mi comida preferida era______________________________ y mi bebida preferida era ______________________________.
4. Yo vivía en ______________________________.
5. Mi libro preferido era______________________________.
6. Mi canción preferida era______________________________.
7. Mi mejor amigo(a) era______________________________.
8. Mi programa de televisión preferido era ______________________________.
9. Mi escuela preferida era ______________________________.
10. Mi pasatiempo favorito era______________________________.

Phrases: describing the past; expressing time relationships
Vocabulary: family members; leisure; sports; studies
Grammar: verbs; imperfect

Vamos a escribir

W9-17 Escriba un ensayo breve sobre su juventud. ¿Cómo era usted cuando tenía diez años? ¿Dónde vivía? ¿Cómo eran sus padres y hermanos? ¿Cómo se divertía usted? ¿Adónde iba? ¿Con quién? Incluya esta información y la información anterior que sea apropiada de arriba en su ensayo. Usted puede agregar más información si quiere.

Cuando yo tenía diez años...

Nombre ______________________ Fecha ______________

Después de escribir

W9-18 Haga una lista de todos los verbos y sujetos que usted usó en su ensayo. Luego escriba el infinitivo y la forma correcta del presente, del imperfecto y del pretérito en el espacio indicado. El primer verbo ya está escrito en la forma correcta.

As you learn more verb tenses in Spanish, it becomes increasingly important to be able to choose among them in your writing. Charts of this type will help you to select the correct verb form. Remember, you will need additional time to acquire the different verb forms in your speech. Be patient with yourself. It is well worth the time and effort!

Infinitivo	Sujeto	Presente	Imperfecto	Pretérito
tener	*yo*	*tengo*	*tenía*	*tuve*

Nombre ______________________________ Fecha ______________

Actividades y ejercicios orales

Pronunciación esencial

CD2-15 Spanish *b* and *v*

In Spanish, **b** and **v** are pronounced the same. Their pronunciation depends on their position in a word or in a group of words.

W9-19 At the beginning of a single word or a group of words (after a pause) and after **m** or **n**, Spanish **b** and **v** are pronounced very much like the *b* in *boy*. Listen to the following sentences and repeat after the speaker.

—**B**uenos días, señorita. **B**usco un regalo para la **b**oda de mis amigos este **v**iernes.
—**B**ueno... un reloj es un **b**uen regalo. Este reloj es muy **b**onito.
—Sí, lo es *(Yes, it is)*... , pero creo que **v**oy a regalarles un álbum para fotos.
—**B**uena idea... así **v**an a recordar su **b**oda para siempre.

CD2-16 **W9-20** In all other positions, particularly between vowels, Spanish **b** and **v** are pronounced softly. To pronounce them correctly, start to say **b**, but at the last moment, do not quite close your lips. Listen to the following sentences and repeat after the speakers.

—¿En qué puedo ser**v**irles, jó**v**enes?
—Buscamos un regalo para nuestra mamá. Su cumpleaños es el sá**b**ado. ¿Nos ayuda, por fa**v**or?
—¡Cómo no! Este brazalete es bonito, ¿no?
—Claro. Pero si hu**b**iera uno menos caro... [Speaker voice trails off]

En contexto

CD2-17 **W9-21 ¡Felices vacaciones de verano!** Escuche la siguiente conversación. Decida si las siguientes oraciones son verdaderas **(V)**, falsas **(F)** o si no hay suficiente información **(N)** para contestar.

1. _____ Los señores Torreón, Alicia y David celebran las Navidades en Chile.
2. _____ La Navidad en Chile se celebra en el verano.
3. _____ En Wisconsin no hace mucho frío en el invierno.
4. _____ A Alicia le gusta nadar en el mar.
5. _____ Alicia y David van a la playa en Viña del Mar.

Nombre ______________________________ Fecha ______________

VOCABULARIO ESENCIAL 

CD2-18 **W9-22 Regalos de Navidad.** Alicia llama a su familia para desearles Feliz Navidad. Alicia y su madre están conversando sobre los regalos de Navidad que se dieron en Santiago y en Madison. Escriba el nombre del regalo que recibió cada uno y quién se lo regaló.

	Regalo(s)	**¿De quién?**
Señora Torreón	______________	______________
Señora Benson	______________	______________
Señor Torreón	______________	______________
Shawn	______________	______________
Miguel	______________	______________
Alicia	______________	______________
David	______________	______________
Señor Benson	______________	______________

CD2-19 **W9-23 Cuando éramos niños.** David y Alicia están hablando sobre su niñez *(childhood)* en Wisconsin. Lea las oraciones de abajo y escuche su conversación. Indique si cada oracion es verdadera **(V)** o falsa **(F)**.

1. _____ Cuando Alicia era niña, jugaba con la nieve.
2. _____ A David no le gustaba esquiar.
3. _____ Alicia y David jugaban en la calle.
4. _____ Nunca practicaban juegos de video.
5. _____ Alicia nadaba todas las mañanas.
6. _____ David veía la televisión.
7. _____ Alicia no tenía bicicleta.
8. _____ Alicia y David se divertían mucho cuando eran niños.

Nombre ______________________ Fecha ____________

PASO 4 De compras

LECCIÓN 10 ¿DESEA ALGO MÁS?

Cuaderno de ejercicios

VOCABULARIO ESENCIAL

W10-1 **¡Adivine qué es!** Aquí hay descripciones de varias frutas, vegetales y carnes. Adivine qué es y escriba el nombre en el espacio en blanco.

Ejemplo: Es rojo, no es dulce *(sweet)*, pero es una fruta. Se come en muchas ensaladas.
el tomate

1. Es una fruta amarilla. Es la fruta favorita de los monos *(monkeys)*.

   ____

2. Es como una naranja, pero es más grande y es amarga *(bitter)*. Se come mucho en el desayuno.

   ____

3. Es un vegetal blanco que se parece mucho al bróculi.

   ____

4. Es un vegetal que da sabor *(flavor)* a muchos platos. Cuando uno lo corta, le hace salir lágrimas *(it makes your eyes teary)*.

   ____

5. Es una fruta roja y se usa para hacer pasteles *(pies)*.

   ____

6. Es un vegetal verde de hojas *(leaves)* que se come en las ensaladas.

   ____

7. Es el vegetal favorito de Bugs Bunny.

   ____

8. Es una fruta pequeña, redonda y roja. Se sirve muchas veces encima de la tarta de queso *(cheesecake)*.

   ____

Nombre ______________________ Fecha ____________

W10-2 **¿Dónde se compra?** A continuación hay cinco tiendas diferentes. Haga una lista de tres o cuatro cosas que se pueden comprar en cada una.

Productos: ______________________

Productos: ______________________

Productos: ______________________

Productos: ______________________

Productos: ______________________

Nombre ______________________ Fecha __________

Gramática esencial

W10-3 Consejos para una entrevista. Susana va a tener una entrevista de trabajo mañana con el señor Navarro en su mercado. Un amigo le da consejos sobre lo que debe y no debe hacer. Use los mandatos informales para hacer oraciones completas.

1. no estar nerviosa

   ____

2. vestirse apropiadamente

   ____

3. responder a cada pregunta

   ____

4. llegar a tiempo a la entrevista

   ____

5. no fumar cigarrillos ni cigarros

   ____

6. no comer nada mientras hablas

   ____

7. mirar directamente al señor Navarro

   ____

8. escribirle una carta para darle las gracias al señor Navarro

   ____

W10-4 En el mercado. Dos amigos están en un mercado de comestibles. Comparan las verduras y las frutas que venden allí. ¿Qué dicen?

Ejemplo: lechuga / estar / caro / bróculi
La lechuga está más cara que el bróculi.

1. plátanos / estar / barato / uvas

   ____

   ____

2. cebolla / estar / fresco / apio *(celery)*

   ____

   ____

3. fresas / estar / dulce / frambuesas *(raspberries)*

____

____

4. naranjas / tener / fibra / manzanas

____

____

5. pimientos / ser / grande / rábanos

____

____

6. espinacas *(spinach)* / ser / nutritivo / zanahorias

____

____

W10-5 Les presento a mi familia. María Alexandra nos va a describir su familia y va a exagerar un poco. Complete la descripción en la próxima página con las palabras apropiadas de la lista siguiente. Usted puede usar una palabra más de una vez y hacer todos los cambios necesarios.

el	tan	trabajador
la	más	guapo
los	menos	simpático
las	mejor	amable
	peor	inteligente
	tanto	ocupado
	mayor	bonito
	menor	bajo
		delicioso
		organizado
		responsable

Nombre ________________________________ Fecha ________________

Mi familia vive en Buenos Aires, Argentina. Mi papá es __________ hombre __________ del mundo. Él es el dueño del __________ mercado pequeño de Buenos Aires. Nuestro mercado es __________ __________ __________ de la calle Independencia. Nuestros precios son __________ __________ __________ de toda la ciudad y nuestras frutas y verduras son __________ __________ __________. Mi mamá nos ayuda con la contabilidad. Ella es contadora y es __________ __________ contadora de Buenos Aires. Mi mamá es __________ __________ como mi papá. También es __________ __________ como él.

Yo trabajo con mi papá en el mercado y hago los pedidos; soy __________ persona __________ __________ del mundo. También estudio negocios por la noche en la universidad y soy muy estudioso. Trato de ser __________ persona __________ __________ de mi clase. Por ahora, tengo muy buenas notas y el mercado está dando ganancias *(profits)*.

W10-6 Consejos. Elena Aguilar está dándoles consejos a sus empleados. ¿Qué les dice? Use mandatos formales.

Ejemplos: La señorita Gómez come sólo postres para el desayuno y no come nada para el almuerzo. De las 3:00 a las 5:00 no puede trabajar porque está cansada.
Señorita Gómez, coma usted fruta para el almuerzo.
o *Desayune bien, señorita Gómez.*

1. Un empleado llega cinco minutos tarde todos los días porque tiene problemas mecánicos con su auto.

____

____

2. Una estudiante que trabaja en la tienda veinte horas a la semana, pasa el tiempo comprando refrescos y hablando con otros empleados todos los días.

____

____

3. Otra empleada descansa cada treinta minutos pero trabaja muy rápido cuando está trabajando.

____

____

4. Una empleada joven siempre está cansada porque sale a bailar y se acuesta tarde tres o cuatro veces a la semana.

____

____

5. Un empleado sólo hace las cosas cuando Elena Aguilar se lo pide dos o tres veces.

____

____

Nombre ______________________ Fecha ______________

W10-7 Qué hacer y qué no hacer durante las horas de trabajo. En el mercado central, la gerente, Elena Aguilar, hizo una lista de mandatos para todos los empleados. Lea la lista siguiente y escriba la lista con mandatos formales en vez de infinitivos.

¡Para todos los empleados!

Por favor, leer y saber las reglas de la empresa

Hacer lo siguiente:

- Llegar a tiempo a su trabajo.
- Lavarse las manos antes de trabajar con la fruta.
- Descansar quince minutos a las 10:00 de la mañana y a las 2:00 de la tarde.
- Comer a las 12:00 en la cafetería o afuera.
- Ser cortés con todos sus compañeros de trabajo.
- Salir del trabajo a las 5:00 en punto de la tarde.
- En caso de emergencia, buscar a la señorita Aguilar en la oficina y decirle qué pasa.

No hacer lo siguiente:

- No llegar tarde al trabajo.
- No hablar con otros empleados sobre su vida personal.
- No cambiar su cheque durante las horas de trabajo.
- No salir temprano sin permiso de la señorita Aguilar.

Hagan lo siguiente:

____

____

____

____

____

____

____

No hagan lo siguiente:

____

____

____

____

Nombre ______________________ Fecha ____________

Cultura

W10-8 Por el mundo hispano. Complete las siguientes oraciones con la información cultural apropiada.

1. En Latinoamérica y en España, muchas personas prefieren comprar comida en ______________________.
2. En una carnicería se compran ______________________.
3. Se compra el pan en ______________________.
4. Hay mejores precios en ______________________.
5. Los productos son más frescos en ______________________.
6. Algunas de las secciones que se encuentran en un mercado son las de ______________________.
7. Si un artículo no tiene precio fijo, se puede ______________________.
8. ¿Dónde es recomendable quedarse si uno está en Buenos Aires? ______________________
9. ¿Qué cosas especiales se puede comprar en Argentina? ______________________
10. ¿Qué se come en un asado? ______________________

W10-9 Lectura. Mire el anuncio en la página siguiente y conteste las siguientes preguntas.

1. ¿Qué se vende en esta tienda? ¿Dónde se encuentra la tienda? ______________________
2. ¿Cuánto cuesta una libra de piernas de pollo? ______________________
3. ¿Cuál es la carne más cara? ¿Cuál es la carne más barata? ______________________
4. Usted necesita dos litros de refrescos, una libra de cebollas verdes, un galón de aceite de maíz y tres libras de carne para asar. ¿Cuánto dinero necesita llevar a la carnicería? ______________________
5. Si usted gasta más de 5 dólares en esta tienda, ¿qué recibe gratis? ______________________

CARNICERIA LA VILLA

"La que no tiene sucursales"

ESPECIALES DE SEMANA SANTA

CARNE PARA ASAR.............. $1.59 *LIBRA*
PIERNAS DE POLLO.............. 49¢ *LIBRA*
PALOMILLA........................... $1.99 *LIBRA*

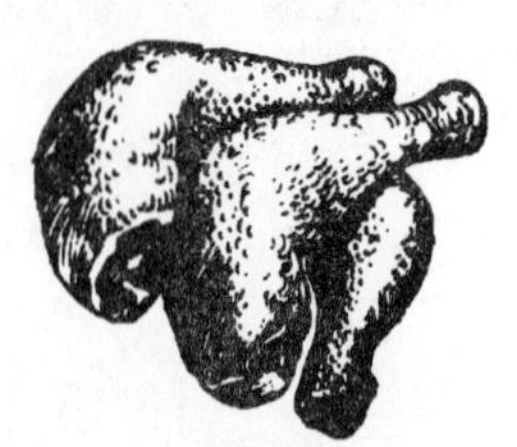

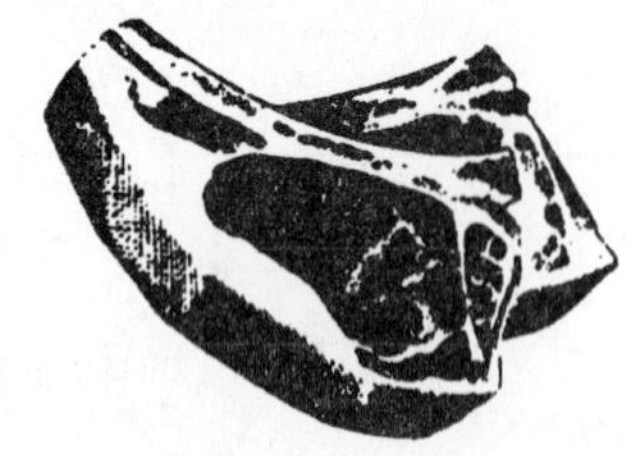

CARNE TIERNA RANCHERA. $2.25 *LIBRA*
MENUDO.............................. 39¢ *LIBRA*
PATITAS DE PUERCO.......... 39¢ *LIBRA*

TAPATIO, 5 oz........................... 2 x 89¢
ACEITE DE MAIZ GALON.................... $4.79
FARAON JALAPEÑO 28 OZ.............. $1.19
GAMESA PASTAS 7 OZ.............. 5 x $1.00
PAPEL BOSIC.............................. 2 x 89¢
SARDINAS ROYAL CROWN 15 OZ...... 99¢
PAN BLANCO.............................. 2 x 89¢
HUEVOS BLANCOS (PAQ. DE 20).......... $1.99
RABANITOS......................... 4 lbs. x $1.00
CEBOLLAS VERDES........... 5 lbs. x $1.00
CILANTRO............................... 5 x $1.00

2214 SO. SAN PEDRO ST., LOS ANGELES, CA 90011

(213) 748-6014

*Con la compra de un mínimo de $5 dólares, reciba una docena de tortillas "La Tapatía"

Nombre ______________________________ Fecha ______________

¡A leer!: Los avisos clasificados

Antes de leer

W10-10 Muchas tiendas que se especializan en la venta de ciertos productos ponen un anuncio *(ad)* en la sección de anuncios clasificados de un periódico. ¿Qué tipo de información sobre los productos se incluye en estos anuncios?

____

____

____

Vamos a leer

W10-11 Examine los anuncios clasificados de esta página y de la página siguiente. Escoja dos anuncios y escriba la siguiente información en los espacios indicados.

Nombre de la tienda	Productos que se venden	Dirección (calle y número)
1. ____________	____________	____________
2. ____________	____________	____________

SECCION ESPECIAL DE AVISO OPORTUNO CLASIFICADO POR TEMAS

TELEFONOS

18•59•28
18•12•45
18•47•51

COMO REDACTAR SU ANUNCIO: 1. SEA CONCRETO. Anuncie sin perderse en detalles, con un texto comprensible, y datos que den una idea clara. 2. SEA VERAZ. Si busca comprar o vender, especifique las condiciones, y realizará su operación con mayor rapidez. La verdad vende. 3. NO OMITA DATOS. Números telefónicos y dirección son muy indispensables. Incluya horarios en los que se le localice.

AVISOS DISPONIBLES: El regular, en mayúsculas y minúsculas, $370 pesos palabra; El DESTACADO, TODAS EN MAYUSCULAS, $390 pesos palabra; EL ESPECIAL, EN MAYUSCULAS o minúsculas, en tipo negro. $480 pesos palabra. TODOS ESTOS PRECIOS YA INCLUYEN EL I.V.A.

LLAME a cualquiera de estos 3 números, de 8 AM a 5 PM, lunes a sábado, y ordene su anuncio. Nuestras operadoras tomarán su orden, se confirmará telefónicamente su inserción, y en su domicilio u negocio recibirá Ud. la factura correspondiente. EN NUESTRAS OFICINAS se reciben avisos de ocasión en el mismo horario.

A/ ANUNCIOS
B/ TRANSPORTE
C/ EMPLEOS
D/ MERCANCIA
E/ RANCHOS
F/ EDICTOS Y OFICIALES
G/ RENTA DE BIENES RAICES
H/ VENTA DE BIENES RAICES
I/ SALONES, FIESTAS, ETC.
J/ SERVICIOS VARIOS

Nombre ______________________________ Fecha ______________

FLORERIA Y REGALOS

"ALI" | "JAZMIN"

MAR DEL NORTE #5117 FOVISSTE TERESIANO | MONTES APENINOS Y SIERRA LEONA # 5479 LA CUESTA

TEL. 16-53-70

Arreglos florales naturales y artificiales para toda ocasión arreglos con globos gigantes, plantas naturales y coronas, especial del mes, decoraciones para bodas o quinceañeras, 78 arreglos naturales, salón, iglesia y carro todo por $495,000.- M.N. aparte el suyo con tiempo ENTREGA GRATIS A DOMICILIO. Atendidos personalmente por su propietaria ALI LUCERO.

E18J-F30J

CARNICERIA

HERMANOS CARDENAS

Le ofrece las mejores carnes, frutas y legumbres. Lo esperamos en Guadiana #5375 entre Suiza y Luxemburgo Col. San Antonio.

E15J-F10A

W10-12 Los símbolos y las letras de las diferentes secciones de los anuncios clasificados indican la clasificación por tema de los anuncios. Conteste las siguientes preguntas sobre estas secciones.

1. Si usted busca trabajo, ¿cuál es la letra y el nombre de la sección que necesita?

   ____

2. ¿En qué sección se encuentran los apartamentos que usted puede rentar?

   ____

3. Imagínese que usted va a vender un televisor que ya no necesita. ¿En qué sección se encuentra su anuncio?

   ____

4. Si usted quiere llamar para poner un anuncio clasificado en el periódico, ¿a qué números puede llamar?

   ____

5. ¿Cuál es el horario para llamar para poner un anuncio? (las horas) de ____________ a ____________ (los días) de ____________ a ____________.

Nombre ______________________________ Fecha ______________

Después de leer

W10-13 Usted va a tener una fiesta especial con mucha comida, un pastel para la ocasión y decoraciones para la mesa y la casa. Con un(a) compañero(a) de clase, escriba una conversación con las llamadas telefónicas a las varias tiendas de los anuncios clasificados para preguntar lo siguiente:

- si la tienda tiene ciertas cosas para su fiesta especial
- el precio de cada cosa
- si la tienda acepta tarjetas de crédito
- dónde está cada tienda

¡A escribir!

Antes de escribir

W10-14 Piense en las publicidades que Ud. ve con frecuencia en las revistas y en los periódicos. Llene la tabla a continuación con información sobre los productos y las publicidades.

Productos	**¿En qué tipo de tienda se vende(n)?**	**¿Quiénes van a comprar este producto?**	**¿Qué mandatos formales se usan en las publicidades?**
Cereal azucarado *(sweetened)*			
Café descafeínado			
Suplementos de calcio *(calcium)*			
Verduras congeladas *(frozen)*			
Helados sin conservantes			
Salsas y especies *(spices)* orientales			
Pan y panecillos frescos			

Phrases: appreciating food
Vocabulary: food: bread, cereals, drinks, fish and seafood, fruits, legumes and vegetables, meat; quantity
Grammar: comparisons: adjectives, equality, inequality; verbs: imperative **usted(es)**

Nombre ______________________ Fecha ______________

Vamos a escribir

W10-15 Usted es dueño(a) de una tienda pequeña y quiere vender más productos. Diseñe y escriba un anuncio para su tienda. Incluya lo siguiente:

- el nombre de su tienda, la dirección y el teléfono
- el tipo de tienda
- qué se vende
- los precios y las ofertas especiales
- dibujos o fotos de sus productos (puede recortarlos de una revista)
- otra información importante

Don´t forget to use formal commands in your ad!

Nombre ______________________ Fecha ______________

Después de escribir

W10-16 Examine el anuncio de un(a) compañero(a) de clase y conteste las siguientes preguntas sobre su anuncio.

1. ¿Cómo se llama la tienda?

 ____

2. ¿Dónde está?

 ____

3. ¿Qué productos se venden en la tienda?

 ____

4. ¿Qué va a comprar usted allí?

 ____

5. ¿Qué productos tienen precios especiales?

 ____

6. ¿Cómo puede usted ahorrar dinero en esa tienda?

 ____

7. ¿Piensa usted volver a esa tienda frecuentemente? ¿Por qué sí o por qué no?

 ____

Nombre ______________________________ Fecha ______________

Actividades y ejercicios orales

En contexto

CD2-20 **W10-17** **¿Desea algo más?** Escuche la siguiente conversación. Decida si las siguientes oraciones son verdaderas **(V)**, falsas **(F)** o si no hay suficiente información **(N)** para contestarlas.

1. _______ El señor Navarro quiere hacer un pedido de vinos para el mercado.
2. _______ Los vinos argentinos son tan buenos como los vinos franceses.
3. _______ En el mercado venden vinos italianos.
4. _______ En este mercado las frutas no son frescas.
5. _______ La idea de vender bebidas y comidas en el mismo lugar es práctica.

Vocabulario esencial

CD2-21 **W10-18** **En la tienda de comestibles.** Usted va a escuchar una conversación entre María Alexandra Navarro y la señora Álvarez, una de sus clientes. Mientras usted escucha la conversación, indique los productos que compra la señora Álvarez.

_______ cebollas

_______ coliflor

_______ fresas

_______ lechuga

_______ manzanas

_______ naranjas

_______ piñas

_______ tomates

_______ uvas

_______ vino blanco

_______ vino tinto

_______ zanahorias

Nombre ______________________ Fecha ______________

CD2-22 **W10-19 El señor Peraza y María Alexandra hacen pedidos para el mercado.** El señor Navarro les va a decir al señor Peraza, su socio, y a María Alexandra varios productos que deben pedir para el mercado. Escuche la siguiente conversación entre el señor Navarro, el señor Peraza y María Alexandra y escriba a continuación los mandatos formales que usted escucha. Incluya los pronombres directos e indirectos cuando sea necesario.

Before you listen to the conversation, review the command forms if you need to. Think about when a person would use a command form and what tone of voice he/she might use.

1. *vayan*
2. ______________________
3. ______________________
4. ______________________
5. ______________________
6. ______________________
7. ______________________
8. ______________________
9. ______________________
10. ______________________

Nombre ______________________ Fecha ____________

LECCIÓN 11 ¡VAMOS DE COMPRAS! ¡QUÉ CHÉVERE!

Cuaderno de ejercicios

VOCABULARIO ESENCIAL

W11-1 Asociaciones. ¿Qué colores asocia usted con los siguientes días festivos o con las siguientes cosas? Escriba los colores abajo.

1. Halloween (el día de las brujas) ____________ y ____________
2. la Navidad ____________ y ____________
3. el día de acción de gracias ____________ y ____________
4. el 4 de julio (en los Estados Unidos) ____________, ____________ y ____________
5. la Coca-Cola ____________ y ____________
6. Los Bulls de Chicago ____________ y ____________
7. La organización "Greenpeace" ____________
8. Pepsi ____________ y ____________
9. las manzanas, los tomates y el vino tinto ____________

W11-2 ¿Qué me voy a poner? Graciela les pregunta a sus amigas Eli y Beatriz qué ropa debe usar en las siguientes situaciones. Dele sugerencias según la situación.

Ejemplo: las montañas para esquiar
unos anteojos de sol, una chaqueta grande, unos guantes

1. la oficina para trabajar

____________, ____________, ____________

2. la playa

____________, ____________, ____________
____

3. de compras con su mamá

____________, ____________, ____________

4. la iglesia

____________, ____________, ____________

Nombre ______________________ Fecha ____________

Gramática esencial

W11-3 ¿Qué harán Beatriz, Graciela y Eli? Graciela, Beatriz y Eli están hablando de su amistad. Se prometen *(They promise each other)* hacer cosas para fortalecer *(to strengthen)* su relación. Escriba la forma correcta de los verbos en el futuro para completar sus promesas.

Ejemplo: (Graciela) Yo las *llamaré* (llamar) más por teléfono.

1. Nosotras nos ____________ (escribir) más mensajes electrónicos.
2. Beatriz y Eli la ____________ (visitar) más a su amiga Graciela.
3. Graciela no ____________ (comprar) un teléfono ccelular para estar en contacto con sus amigo.
4. Graciela, Beatriz y Eli ____________ (divertirse) juntas.
5. Beatriz ____________ (invitar) a casa a Eli y a Graciela para comer.

W11-4 Amiga mandona *(Bossy friend)*. ¿Qué quiere Beatriz que hagan sus amigas Eli y Graciela? Escriba oraciones completas, usando las frases de abajo.

Ejemplo: (Eli) hacer más ejercicios
Beatriz quiere que Eli haga más ejercicios.

1. (Eli) descansar mucho más en Caracas

____

2. (Graciela) pasar más tiempo con ella y Eli

____

3. (Graciela) ir al cine con ellas el viernes

____

4. (Eli) no comprar tantos recuerdos

____

5. (Eli) no correr a toda hora

____

W11-5 Deseos y preocupaciones. Beatriz está hablando con sus amigas Graciela y Eli sobre sus deseos y preocupaciones *(worries)*. Escriba oraciones, usando las siguientes palabras y frases. Haga los cambios necesarios y fíjese bien en si se debe usar el infinitivo o el subjuntivo.

Remember to use the subjunctive here only *if there is a change of subject after the verb* ***querer.*** *Check your completed sentences and make sure that all words are in agreement.*

1. yo / querer pasar / más tiempo con ustedes

____

____

2. mi / padres / querer / que yo / pasar / más tiempo en casa

____

____

3. mi / mamá / querer / que yo / limpiar / mi / dormitorio / todos los días

____

____

4. yo / querer / que ella / me / ayudar

____

____

5. ¡yo / sólo / querer / ser / feliz!

____

____

CULTURA

W11-6 Por el mundo hispano. Lea las siguientes oraciones. Si la oración es cierta, escriba **Sí** en el espacio indicado. Si la oración es falsa, escriba **No.**

1. _______ Carolina Herrera es una pintora famosa de Venezuela.
2. _______ La ropa y los acesorios de Carolina Herrera son populares en muchos países, incluso en los Estados Unidos.
3. _______ Carolina Herrera no quiere que su hija trabaje en su compañía.

W11-7 Lectura. Lea el artículo en la página siguiente sobre un desfile de modas de ropa deportiva y conteste las siguientes preguntas con oraciones completas.

1. ¿Qué tipo de ropa se presenta en el artículo y en las fotos de la página siguiente?

____

2. ¿Dónde hizo Dana la presentación?

____

3. ¿Para qué deporte es la ropa?

____

4. ¿En qué país se hizo la presentación?

____

5. Para una presentación de nuevos diseños se necesitan diseñadores, anfitriones (las personas que hacen las preparaciones y pagan el costo) e invitados. ¿Quiénes fueron los anfitriones? ¿Quiénes fueron los invitados?

____

____

DANA Y SU ROPA DEPORTIVA

Fotos: Hugo García Tapia

Dana ha diseñado para los hombres y las mujeres que gustan del deporte una línea de prendas y accesorios inspirados en el diseño italiano: playeras, shorts, calcetas, tines, muñequeras y testieri.

El Club Atlético del Hotel Nikko fue la "cancha" donde Dana presentó su colección primavera-verano de ropa y accesorios deportivos. Las prendas de vestir y los accesorios tienen como color fundamental el blanco, con estampado de muñecos para las activas damas y figuras geométricas para los varones. Los modelos se inspiran en el diseño italiano y, a pesar de que han sido pensados para practicar tenis, dada su comodidad y elegancia se pueden emplear para cualquier otro deporte, e incluso para quien gusta vestir a diario sport. Los anfitriones fueron el Sr. Moiz Dana y su hijo, el Ing. Alberto Dana, y entre los invitados estaban representantes de los mejores almacenes.

Llegan a México las prendas deportivas y los accesorios que están de moda entre los europeos.

estar de moda *to be in style*

¡A leer!: Baron's

Antes de leer

W11-8 Cuando usted mira los anuncios para las tiendas de ropa en el periódico, ¿qué tipo de información busca? ¿Qué tipo de información es importante?

____

____

____

____

____

Vamos a leer

W11-9 Mire el anuncio para el almacén *(department store)* Baron's en la página siguiente y conteste las siguientes preguntas.

1. ¿El almacén Baron's tiene solamente ropa para hombres, o también para mujeres?

   ____

2. ¿En qué estación del año ocurrió *(happened)* esta venta?

   ____

3. Lea las siguientes oraciones sobre el anuncio de Baron's. Escriba **Sí** en el espacio indicando si la oración es verdadera o **No** si la oración es falsa.

   a. _______ Baron's tiene una amplia *(wide)* selección de blusas.

   b. _______ Todos los pantalones están en venta *(are on sale)*.

   c. _______ Hay una amplia selección de trajes.

   d. _______ Hay un selecto grupo de camisas de sport de famosos diseñadores *(designers)*.

   e. _______ Baron's ofrece hacer alteraciones gratis *(free)*.

   f. _______ Baron's no abre los domingos.

Nombre ______________________ Fecha ______________

VENTA DE VERANO EN BARON'S

15% a 50% Desc.

AHORRE 15% a 50%

En Una Amplia Selección de Diseñadores

Trajes & Chaquetes de Sport

Marcas : Christian Dior
Lanvin • Pierre Cardin
Givenchy • Adolfo • Marco
Finchley • Oleg Cassini
Groshire • Profilo
Charles Jourdan • Diplomat
... y muchos más

TODOS LOS PANTALONES DE LA TIENDA ESTAN EN

VENTA

Diseños en Mangas Corta y Larga

Camisas de Sport

Y en Selecto Grupo de Famosos Diseñadores

Camisas de Sport

Marcas de: Givenchy,
Alan Stuart, Dior,
David Michaels, D'Avila,
Cassini, Damon,
Louis Azzaro, Lanvin
... y más

Regular hasta $32.50

AHORA $19.99

Naturalmente, Alteraciones Gratis por Expertos

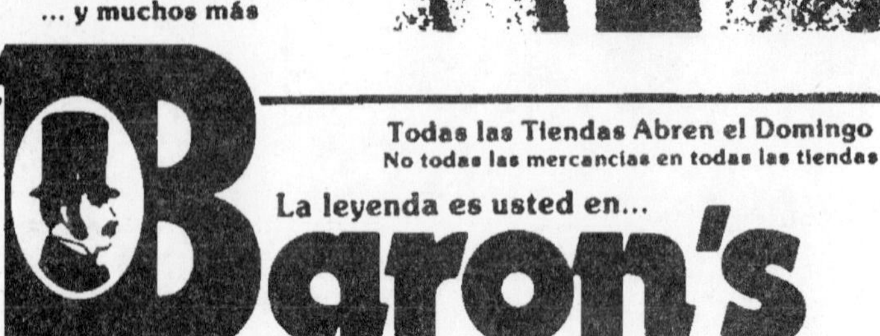

La Cadena de Tienda Mayor de la Florida desde 1945, en Ropas para Caballeros.
Dadeland • Miami International Mall • Westland • 445 Lincoln Road Mall • Bal Harbour Shops
The Mall at 163rd Street • Broward Mall • The Galleria • Pompano Square • Coral Square
Boynton Beach Mall • Palm Beach Mall • Altamonte Mall • Florida Mall

Nombre ______________________________ Fecha ______________

Después de leer

W11-10 Escriba un anuncio de publicidad para una tienda, anunciando los artículos de ropa en venta, los precios y los diseñadores. ¿En qué fecha es la venta y qué días y a qué horas se abre la tienda?

¡A escribir!

Antes de escribir

W11-11 Complete las siguientes oraciones con información personal sobre su ropa.

1. Para ir al cine con mis amigos, me gusta ponerme ______________ de color ______________.
2. Cuando tengo que lavar el auto, llevo ______________ de color ______________.
3. El primer día de clase generalmente me pongo ______________________________.
4. Cuando practico algún deporte o pasatiempo, prefiero llevar ______________________________.
5. Cuando voy a cenar en un restaurante elegante, me gusta llevar ______________________________.

Nombre ______________________ Fecha __________

W11-12 Conteste las siguientes preguntas con oraciones completas.

1. Generalmente, ¿cuánto paga usted por un par de zapatos?

   ____

2. ¿Le gusta ir a las tiendas por la mañana, por la tarde o por la noche? ¿Por qué?

   ____

3. ¿Por cuánto tiempo le gusta estar en las tiendas?

   ____

4. En su ciudad, ¿en qué calle hay muchos almacenes o tiendas?

   ____

Phrases: describing objects; talking about past events; writing a letter (informal)
Vocabulary: clothing; colors
Grammar: verbs; irregular preterite; preterite

Vamos a escribir

W11-13 Eli Miller compró varias cosas en la gran apertura *(grand opening)* de la tienda Gisel's. Cuando llegó a casa de Beatriz, puso todas sus cosas en la sala y le escribió un recado *(message)* a la mamá de su amiga. Escriba el recado que Eli le dejó a la mamá de Beatriz y haga lo siguiente:

- Describa cada prenda de ropa *(article of clothing)* e incluya su precio (en bolívares).
- Mencione por qué Eli compró cada prenda.
- Incluya las cosas que Eli compró para los otros miembros de su familia.

Querida señora Arreaza:

¡Mire lo que compré en la gran apertura de Gisel's!

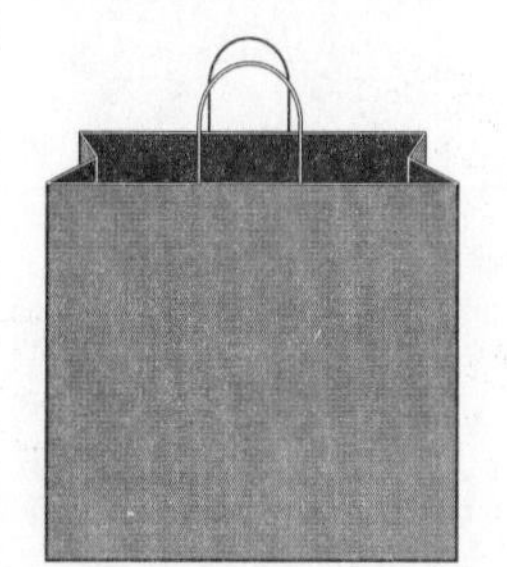

Gracias, y perdone el desorden,

Eli

Perdone el desorden. *Sorry about the mess.*

Después de escribir

W11-14 Dele su recado a un(a) compañero(a) de clase. Luego examinen juntos los dos recados y hagan lo siguiente.

1. Subrayen *(Underline)* todos los sustantivos que hay en el recado.
2. Tracen *(Draw)* un círculo alrededor de cada adjetivo.
3. ¿Concuerdan *(Agree)* los adjetivos con los sustantivos? Si no, corríjanlos.
4. Tracen un cuadro alrededor de cada verbo.
5. Si un verbo está en el tiempo presente, escriban **pres.** arriba del verbo. Si un verbo está en el tiempo pretérito, escriban **pret.** arriba del verbo.
6. Examinen todos los verbos usados. ¿Escogieron ustedes el tiempo verbal correcto? Si no, corríjanlos.

Ejemplo: La blusa es (*pres.*) muy bonita, ¿no?

Nombre ______________________ Fecha ____________

Actividades y ejercicios orales

EN CONTEXTO

CD2-23 **W11-15** **¡Qué chévere!** Escuche la siguiente conversación. Decida si las siguientes oraciones son verdaderas **(V)**, falsas **(F)** o si no hay suficiente información **(N)** para contestar.

1. _____ Eli y Beatriz van a ir a una tienda de ropa.
2. _____ La tienda está en Caracas.
3. _____ Eli necesita ropa para ir a fiestas.
4. _____ Eli tiene mucho dinero para comprar ropa.
5. _____ La ropa en Caracas es más económica que en los Estados Unidos.

VOCABULARIO ESENCIAL

CD2-24 **W11-16** **Las compras de Eli (Primera parte).** Eli fue de compras a una tienda que tenía una oferta *(sale)*. Cuando salió de la tienda, su amiga Beatriz le hizo varias preguntas sobre sus compras. Complete el cuadro con la información que ella le dio.

	¿Para quién?	**Artículo de ropa**	**Color**	**Uso (¿Para qué es?)**
1.	____________	____________	____________	____________
2.	____________	____________	____________	____________
3.	____________	____________	____________	____________
4.	____________	____________	____________	____________

CD2-25 **W11-17** **Las compras de Eli (Segunda parte).** Ahora usted va a oír cinco oraciones basadas en la conversación de Beatriz y Eli. Después de escuchar cada oración dos veces, escriba **V** si es verdadera o **F** si es falsa.

1. _____
2. _____
3. _____
4. _____
5. _____

W11-18 De compras. Usted va a escuchar una conversación entre una dependiente y su cliente. Mientras usted escucha la conversación, complete la siguiente información con lo que compra la cliente.

Artículo de ropa: ______________________________

Color: ______________________________

Talla: ______________________________

Precio: ______________________________

LECCIÓN 12 ¡QUÉ DELICIOSO EL CAFÉ!

Cuaderno de ejercicios

VOCABULARIO ESENCIAL

W12-1 ¡Tantas cosas que hacer! Gloria está haciendo varias actividades en su viaje de negocios. Escriba una conversación que corresponda a cada dibujo.

Ejemplo: En la agencia de carros

Gloria: *¿Puedo alquilar un auto económico en Bogotá?*

Empleado: *Sí, señora, puedo llamar a nuestra compañía y reservar un auto económico.*

Gloria: *Muchas gracias.*

1. En el banco

Empleado: ______________________________

____

____

Gloria: ______________________________

____

____

Empleado: ______________________________

____

____

2. En la oficina de correos

Gloria: ______________________

____

____

Empleada: ______________________

____

____

Gloria: ______________________

____

____

W12-2 Preguntas personales. Conteste las siguentes preguntas personales, usando oraciones completas. Use el vocabulario de la **Lección 12** para sus respuestas.

El dinero

1. ¿Prefiere usted pagar al contado o con cheque?

____

2. ¿Dónde tiene usted una cuenta de ahorros?

____

3. ¿Dónde está la oficina de correos más cerca de usted?

____

4. ¿Por qué es una buena idea invertir dinero?

____

5. ¿Qué gastos tiene usted?

____

6. En este país, ¿dónde puede usted cambiar un cheque?

____

Los sentimientos

1. ¿De qué se preocupa usted más?

____

2. ¿De qué se quejan más sus profesores?

____

3. ¿De qué se alegra usted frecuentemente?

____

4. ¿Qué le gusta que hagan para usted sus mejores amigos?

____

Nombre ______________________________ Fecha ______________

Gramática esencial

W12-3 Las preocupaciones de la mamá de Gloria. La mamá de Gloria le habla a su hija sobre sus opiniones con respecto al viaje a Bogotá. Complete las siguientes oraciones con la forma correcta del verbo.

Ejemplo: Me gusta que ustedes (ir) en avión.
Me gusta que ustedes vayan en avión.

1. Ojalá que ________________ (hacer) buen tiempo durante su visita.
2. Me alegro que ustedes ________________ (tomar) unos días de vacaciones.
3. Siento mucho que tú ________________ (tener) que regresar tan pronto a Medellín para trabajar.
4. Espero que tus tíos te ________________ (llamar) por teléfono.
5. Me preocupa que ustedes no ________________ (ver) a tus abuelos desde hace tanto tiempo.

W12-4 Preparaciones para el viaje a Bogotá. Enrique y Gloria están haciendo los planes finales para su viaje a Bogotá. Enrique le habla a Gloria sobre sus emociones y opiniones. ¿Qué le dice a ella?

Ejemplo: es importante / tú y yo / estar de acuerdo con todas las decisiones
Es importante que tú y yo estemos de acuerdo con todas las decisiones.

1. (yo) esperar / (tú) / ir a comprar los regalos para tu familia
____
____
2. (yo) preocuparse de / (tú) / trabajar mucho en la hacienda de café
____
____
3. (yo) esperar / (nosotros) / ir juntos a decirles adiós a mis padres
____
____
4. (yo) / alegrarse de / (tú) / estar contenta porque vamos por una semana a Bogotá
____
____
5. es una lástima / (nosotros) / no poder quedarnos más días en Bogotá
____
____

Nombre ______________________ Fecha ____________

W12-5 Las opiniones de Gloria. Gloria reacciona a los comentarios de su mamá. ¿Cuál es su opinión?

Ejemplo: Es mejor que...
Es mejor que nosotros vayamos en avión.

1. Es posible que....
______________________________.
2. Es importante que...
______________________________.
3. Es triste que...
______________________________.
4. Es importante que...
______________________________.
5. Es una lástima que...
______________________________.

W12-6 Querida Gloria. Enrique León regresó de Bogotá y se fue para los Estados Unidos. Enrique le escribió una postal a Gloria desde Miami. Indique la forma correcta de los verbos entre paréntesis.

Querida Gloria,
Me alegro de (estoy / esté / estar) aquí en Miami y siento mucho que tú no (puedes / puedas / poder) estar aquí conmigo. La ciudad de Miami (es / está / ser) muy bonita y el tiempo (es / está / ser) fresco. Espero que tú (vienes / vengas / venir) conmigo en el próximo viaje de negocios. Ojalá que (puedes / puedas / poder) pagar todas las cuentas con el dinero que depositamos en la cuenta corriente. Espero que tú no (tienes / tengas / tener) muchos problemas en la compañía ahora que yo no estoy. Bueno, espero (veo / vea / verte) muy pronto.

Con amor,
Enrique

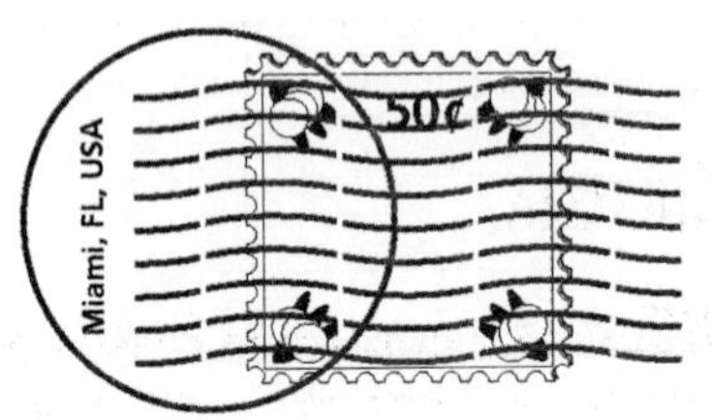

Sra. Gloria León
Calle 12–14, N° 39
Medellín, Colombia
SurAmérica

Nombre ______________________ Fecha ____________

W12-7 Las cosas que veo en mi vida diaria. Exprese sus opiniones y actitudes sobre situaciones o cosas que usted observa en su vida diaria.

1. Es importante que los estudiantes de esta universidad
______________________.
______________________.
2. En la cafetería de la universidad es bueno que
______________________.
______________________.
3. Es imposible que todos los profesores
______________________.
______________________.
4. Es ridículo que no todos los administradores de la universidad
______________________.
______________________.
5. Es lógico que los cursos de los estudiantes
______________________.
______________________.

Cultura

W12-8 Por el mundo hispano. Escriba la mejor respuesta posible para las siguientes preguntas. Busque la información en las lecturas sobre cultura que aparecen en el texto.

1. ¿En qué lugares *(places)* puede uno cambiar dinero en Latinoamérica y España?
____
2. ¿Dónde recibe uno el mejor cambio?
____
3. ¿Qué documento de identificación es mejor usar cuando uno quiere cambiar dinero?
____
4. ¿Qué es el Fondo Monetario Internacional?
____
5. ¿Cuál es su propósito?
____

Nombre ______________________ Fecha ______________

¡A leer!: ¡Suscríbase hoy!

Antes de leer

W12-9 Imagínese que usted quiere suscribirse a una revista. ¿Qué información necesita incluir en el formulario?

____

____

____

Vamos a leer

¡SÍ, QUIERO SUSCRIBIRME!
Y RECIBIR EN MI CASA 6 EJEMPLARES DE
GEOMUNDO
¡Un panorama del mundo a todo color!
POR SOLO $12.60
AHORRE UN 30% DEL PRECIO DE PORTADA
OFERTA ESPECIAL

RECIBA EN SU CASA
BUENHOGAR
La revista para la joven mujer de hogar
12 ejemplares por sólo $23.00
¡Suscríbame hoy!
AHÓRRESE UN 35% DEL PRECIO DE PORTADA

¡SÍ, QUIERO SUSCRIBIRME!
Y RECIBIR EN MI CASA
MUNDO 21
6 numeros por $ 9.97 (15% de descuento)
12 numeros por $17.97 (23% de descuento)
AHORRE HASTA UN 23% DEL PRECIO DE PORTADA
Nombre ______
Dirección ______
Ciudad ______
Estado ______
Z Postal ______

RECIBE EN TU CASA
TU internacional
Tu revista . . . ¡te ayuda a triunfar!
6 ejemplares por sólo $10.50
¡Suscríbete hoy!
AHORRESE UN 30%
Nombre ______
Dirección ______
Ciudad ______ Estado ______ Z Postal ______
Incluyo mi ☐ CHEQUE o ☐ GIRO POSTAL
Cargar a mi ☐ VISA ☐ MASTERCARD
Tarjeta No. ☐☐☐☐☐☐☐☐☐☐☐☐☐☐☐☐☐☐☐☐☐☐☐☐☐
Fecha de Vencimiento ______ Mes ______ Año
Firma autorizada ______
Esta oferta es válida SOLO PARA NUEVAS SUSCRIPCIONES, en Estados Unidos y Puerto Rico.
Hacer cheque o giro postal a nombre de EDITORIAL AMERICA, S.A.
Su primer ejemplar sera puesto en correo dentro de ocho semanas
TUM J0209

Nombre ______________________________ Fecha ______________

W12-10 Conteste las siguientes preguntas sobre la información de la página anterior.

1. Complete el cuadro siguiente con la información que se le pide.

Nombre de la revista	Precio de la suscripción	Número de ejemplares *(copies)*	% de ahorro
a. ______	______	______	______
b. ______	______	______	______
c. ______	______	______	______
d. ______	______	______	______

2. ¿Qué suscripción es la más barata por ejemplar?

____

3. ¿Qué información personal tiene que completar para recibir su suscripción?

____

4. Si usted paga con tarjeta de crédito, ¿qué otra información necesita escribir?

____

5. ¿Cuándo va a recibir usted su primero ejemplar de *TÚ*?

____

6. ¿Qué frases se encuentran en los formularios que motivan a comprar una suscripción?

____

Después de leer

W12-11 Imagínese que usted es editor(a) y está planeando varios artículos para las revistas indicadas a continuación. Escriba los nombres de los artículos en los espacios indicados.

GeoMundo

1. ______________________________
2. ______________________________

Buenhogar

1. ______________________________
2. ______________________________

Mundo21

1. ______________________________
2. ______________________________

TÚ

1. ______________________________
2. ______________________________

Nombre ______________________________ Fecha ______________

¡A escribir!

Antes de escribir

W12-12 Enrique y Gloria van a Bogotá y tienen que hacer un presupuesto porque sus gastos van a ser más altos que en Medellín.

1. Haga una lista de todas las cosas que van a tener que comprar para todos los miembros de la familia de Enrique en Bogotá.

Papá	Mamá	Los hermanos		
		Olga	Mildred	Juan Carlos

2. ¿Cuánto cuestan las cosas mencionadas en la lista anterior en Colombia? Adivine *(Guess)* los precios y escríbalos al lado de cada cosa que Gloria quiere comprar para su familia.

Vamos a escribir

W12-13 Enrique y Gloria tienen que tomar una decisión sobre sus gastos en Bogotá para comprar regalos para su familia. A continuación, escriba una conversación entre Enrique y Gloria. Al final del diálogo los dos tienen que ponerse de acuerdo.

Enrique: ______________________________

Gloria: ______________________________

Enrique: ______________________________

Gloria: ______________________________

Enrique: ______________________________

Gloria: ______________________________

Después de escribir

W12-14 Comparta su conversación con un(a) compañero(a) de clase y entre los dos, practíquenla para presentársela al resto de la clase.

Phrases: agreeing and disagreeing; apologizing; asking and giving advice; asking the price; persuading

Grammar: verbs: subjunctive with **ojalá;** subjunctive with **que**

Actividades y ejercicios orales

En contexto

CD2-27 **W12-15** **¡Qué delicioso el café!** Escuche la siguiente conversación. Decida si las siguientes oraciones son verdaderas **(V)**, falsas **(F)** o si no hay suficiente información **(N)** para contestar.

1. _____ Gloria va a visitar a su familia en Bogotá.
2. _____ Gloria y Enrique van a Bogotá por dos semanas.
3. _____ Ellos trabajan mucho en la hacienda de café.
4. _____ Enrique va a los Estados Unidos a vender café.
5. _____ Enrique va a quedarse cuatro semanas en la Florida.

Vocabulario esencial

CD2-28 **W12-16** **¡Tenemos muchas cosas que hacer!** Enrique y Gloria León están preparándose para ir a Bogotá. Hicieron algunas cosas pero todavía tienen que hacer otras. En la lista que ellos prepararon, indique qué cosas hicieron, marcando **sí**, y qué cosas no han hecho todavía, marcando **no.**

	sí	*no*
1. terminar de preparar el café para las próximas dos semanas		
2. comprar los boletos de avión		
3. comprarle regalos a la familia		
4. visitar a los padres de Enrique para decirles adiós		
5. lavar la ropa		
6. limpiar la casa		
7. llamar el taxi para que venga a buscarlos		

Nombre ______________________________ Fecha ______________

CD2-29 **W12-17** **En el banco.** Escuche la narración e indique la mejor respuesta para completar cada oración.

_____ 1. Enrique y Gloria necesitan cambiar pesos por...
  a. pesos colombianos.
  b. dólares.
  c. bolívares.

_____ 2. Para Miami, Enrique necesita comprar...
  a. cheques personales.
  b. cheques de la cuenta de ahorros.
  c. cheques de viajero.

_____ 3. Enrique y Gloria pagan sus cuentas haciendo cheques de...
  a. la cuenta corriente.
  b. la cuenta de ahorros.
  c. la cuenta de crédito.

_____ 4. Cuando vaya a Bogotá, Gloria no quiere usar...
  a. sus cheques personales.
  b. sus cheques de viajero.
  c. su tarjeta de crédito.

CD2-30 **W12-18** **Exprese su opinión.** El señor Antakly es el gerente general de una empresa de café y sus empleados tienen muchos problemas. Después de escuchar las tres situaciones siguientes de sus empleados, exprese la recomendación del señor Antakly.

Ejemplo: **Empleado:** Señor Antakly, no me siento bien. Comí demasiada pizza. ¿Qué me recomienda usted?
Señor Antakly: *Le recomiendo que vaya al médico.*
o *Le recomiendo que descanse en casa.*

1. ______________________________
2. ______________________________
3. ______________________________

PASO 5 ¡Buen viaje!

LECCIÓN 13 ¡TE ESPERAMOS EN GALICIA!

Cuaderno de ejercicios

VOCABULARIO ESENCIAL

W13-1 Cuando yo viajo... Completa las siguientes oraciones con la palabra apropiada de la lista siguiente.

1. Cuando yo viajo, normalmente pido una (llave / lámpara / habitación) sencilla.
2. No me gusta subir las escaleras *(stairs)*, así que me gustan los hoteles que tienen (ascensor / habitación / reserva).
3. Prefiero un hotel que no sea muy caro, así que si los (recepción / televisor / muebles) son un poco viejos, no me importa.
4. ¡Necesito mi privacidad! Necesito (cocina / cuarto de baño / mesa pequeña) privado(a).
5. Hay mucho ruido en las calles, así que prefiero los cuartos que no dan (a la izquierda / a la calle / recto).
6. Cuando hace mucho calor, me gusta tener (papel higiénico / el espejo / aire acondicionado) en el cuarto.

W13-2 ¿En qué puedo servirle? Su mejor amigo(a) y usted están en la recepción de un hotel en Madrid. En la próxima página, escriba una conversación entre usted y el (la) recepcionista del hotel con los siguientes elementos.

Cliente:	**Recepcionista:**
1. dar un saludo apropiado	2. responder al saludo
3. pedir un cuarto para usted y su amigo(a)	4. preguntar cuántos días, qué tipo de cuarto
5. responder por cuántos días, qué quiere en el cuarto	6. preguntar qué más quiere en el cuarto
7. pedir información sobre precios, restaurantes, dónde cambiar el dinero	8. responder a las preguntas del (de la cliente)
9. darle las gracias al (a la) recepcionista	10. darle la bienvenida a su cliente

Nombre ______________________ Fecha ____________

Cliente: ______________________
Recepcionista: ______________________
Cliente: ______________________
Recepcionista: ______________________
Cliente: ______________________
Recepcionista: ______________________
Cliente: ______________________
Recepcionista: ______________________
Cliente: ______________________
Recepcionista: ______________________

GRAMÁTICA ESENCIAL

W13-3 Optimistas y pesimistas. Normalmente la gente pesimista tiene más dudas que la gente optimista. Escriba oraciones completas que expresen las opiniones de algunos amigos de Ileana.

1. **Tomás:** dudo que Europa / ser más bonita que Panamá, pero creo que el continente europeo / tener muchos lugares interesantes para los turistas

____
____
____

2. **Luis:** es dudoso que los hoteles en Europa / estar baratos, pero no dudo que / haber muchos hoteles allá

____
____
____

3. **Alicia:** no creo que los demás europeos *(other Europeans)* / trabajar tanto como los españoles / creo que los españoles / trabajar más horas

____
____
____

4. **Luis:** no estoy seguro de que / poderse ver Europa en quince días / ¿se necesitan más días?

____
____
____

5. **Teresa:** tal vez / costar mucho dinero viajar por Europa, pero no estoy segura de eso

____
____
____

W13-4 Hablando de festivales. A Manuel y Victoria Castro les gustan las fiestas de Santiago de Compostela. Complete la sigueinte conversación, usando apropiadamente el indicativo o el subjuntivo de los verbos de la lista de abajo. Se puede usar un verbo más de una vez.

haber
hacer

invitar
ir

ser
tener

venir
vivir

Manuel: No hay ningún festival que ____________ igual a las fiestas de Santiago de Compostela, ¿verdad?

Victoria: Ese festival ____________ el más interesante para mí, pero quizás ____________ otros muy buenos aquí en España y en otros países de Europa.

Manuel: Sí, por ejemplo, algún día quiero ir a celebrar la Semana Santa en Sevilla. Se dice que ____________ gente de todas partes del mundo para celebrarla.

Victoria: Conozco a alguien que ____________ a la Semana Santa el próximo año. Se llama María Aquino, y ____________ en Caracas, Venezuela. Tal vez nos ____________ una invitación para visitarla porque ____________ una persona muy generosa.

Manuel: ¡Ojalá que ella nos ____________ a Venezuela algún día también!

W13-5 ¡A comer! Manuel y Victoria están limpiando la casa para la visita de Ileana, pero Victoria tiene mucha hambre. Manuel la invita a comer en un restaurante de la ciudad. Lea la siguiente conversación y decida si se debe usar el indicativo, el subjuntivo o el infinitivo del verbo indicado.

Victoria: Manuel, ¿cuándo (vamos / vayamos / ir) al restaurante? Tengo mucha hambre.
Manuel: Vamos al restaurante inmediatamente antes de limpiar para que (puedes / puedas / poder) comer.
Victoria: Pero, Manuel, no podemos ir al restaurante antes de que nosotros (terminamos / terminemos / terminar) de limpiar la casa.
Manuel: Bueno, ya vamos a (terminamos / terminemos / terminar).
Victoria: Ojalá que a Ileana le (gusta / guste / gustar) nuestra casa y Santiago de Compostela.
Manuel: Claro que sí, Victoria. No te preocupes. Tan pronto como ella (llega / llegue / llegar) a nuestra ciudad, todo le va a (gusta / guste / gustar) mucho.

Nombre ______________________________ Fecha ______________

Cultura

W13-6 Por el mundo hispano. Escriba la letra de la respuesta apropiada para completar cada frase.

a. tiene pocas habitaciones.
b. dejan su pasaporte con el recepcionista.
c. escriben el número del pasaporte en el
d. ofrece habitaciones y desayuno.
e. la mayoría viaja de una ciudad a otra en tren.
f. muchas veces es un castillo.
g. ofrece una cama, más tres comidas.
h. existe un sistema excelente de autobuses.
i representa lo mejor y lo más caro.
j. es el modo más barato de alojarse en España.

1. Un hostal residencia...
2. Una pensión completa...
3. En España, los viajeros... formulario de registro.
4. Acampar...
5. En Latinoamérica...
6. Un hotel de cinco estrellas...
7. En España...
8. Una pensión...
9. En Latinoamérica, los viajeros...
10. Un parador...

Nombre ________________________ Fecha ____________

¡A leer!: España en los paradores

Antes de leer

W13-7 Muchas veces las agencias de viajes ofrecen paquetes que incluyen varias excursiones y actividades, así como el costo del vuelo y alojamiento en diferentes hoteles. Imagínese que un turista visita la ciudad donde usted vive. En el cuadro siguiente, describa un itinerario de un día para este turista. ¿Qué lugares turísticos va a visitar? ¿Dónde va a desayunar, almorzar, cenar? ¿Cómo se llama su hotel? ¿Qué otras excursiones y actividades se incluyen en el paquete?

Por la mañana	Por la tarde	Por la noche

Nombre ______________________ Fecha ____________

Vamos a leer

W13-8 Mire el itinerario de "España en los paradores" en la página siguiente y conteste estas preguntas.

1. ¿Adónde es y cuántos días incluye?

   ____

2. ¿Cuánto cuesta el viaje si usted sale en avión de Nueva York? __________ ¿Y si sale de Miami?

   ____

3. ¿Adónde llega el avión? ______________________

   ¿De dónde sale cuando termina la excursión? ______________________

4. ¿Cuántos días está el viajero en Madrid? __________ ¿Y en Sevilla? __________

5. ¿En qué ciudades hay alojamiento en los paradores?

   _____ Madrid
   _____ Toledo
   _____ Córdoba
   _____ Granada
   _____ Costa del Sol
   _____ Sevilla
   _____ Mérida
   _____ Salamanca
   _____ Bayona
   _____ Cambados
   _____ Santiago de Compostela
   _____ León

6. ¿En qué fechas puede usted ir a España con ese itinerario?

Nombre ______________________ Fecha ____________

España en los Paradores

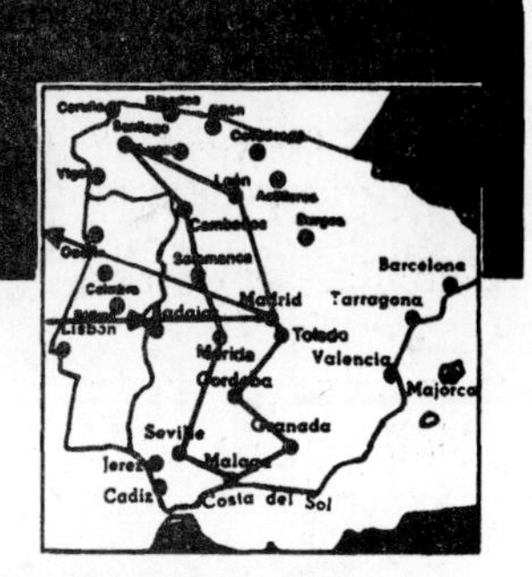

15 DIAS

INCLUYE:

- Avión Jet de ida y regreso.
- 13 noches alojamiento en hoteles de primera y Paradores Nacionales.
- Desayuno diario y 7 comidas.
- Recorrido en ómnibus de lujo.
- Impuestos y servicio de hoteles.
- Tarjeta de descuento en restaurantes y tiendas.
- Traslado y entrada al Gran Casino de Madrid.

Dia 1– RUMBO A ESPAÑA.
Salida en vuelo intercontinental con destino a Madrid.

Dia 2 – MADRID
Llegada a Madrid. Resto del día libre para recorrer la ciudad, sus típicas calles y sus tascas. Alojamiento.

Dia 3– MADRID - TOLEDO - CORDOBA
Salida por la mañana hacia Toledo, visita de la ciudad, la Catedral y la Iglesia de Santo Tomé. Continuación hacia Bailén y Córdoba. Llegada. Cena y alojamiento en el Parador Nacional.

Dia 4– CORDOBA - GRANADA
Desayuno. Visita de la ciudad, su famosa Mezquita, con el laberinto de columnas; el barrio Judío y la Sinagoga. Por la tarde, salida a Granada. Llegada. Cena y alojamiento en el hotel junto a los jardines de la Alhambra.

Dia 5– GRANADA - COSTA DEL SOL
Desayuno. Por la mañana, visita de esta maravillosa ciudad, situada al pie de Sierra Nevada. La incomparable Alhambra, palacio moro, rodeado de jardines y el Generalife. Por la tarde, salida hacia las playas más conocidas en toda Europa, la Costa del Sol. Alojamiento en el hotel.

Dia 6– COSTA DEL SOL - SEVILLA
Desayuno. Salida hacia Ronda, con su famoso Tajo. Arcos de la Frontera y Jérez. Llegada a Sevilla. Alojamiento en el hotel.

Dia 7 – SEVILLA
Desayuno. Visita de la ciudad, con su famosa Catedral, la Torre de la Giralda, el Alcázar, barrio de Santa Cruz, la Torre de Oro. Tarde libre. Alojamiento en el hotel.

Dia 8 – SEVILLA - MERIDA
Desayuno. Salida hacia Zafra en tierras de Extremadura. Llegada a Mérida. Por la tarde, visita de su famoso Teatro Romano. Cena y alojamiento en el Parador Nacional.

Dia 9 – MERIDA - SALAMANCA
Desayuno. Salida hacia Cáceres. Recorrido por la ciudad vieja. Continuación a Hervas y Salamanca. Por la tarde, recorrido de la ciudad, su famosa Plaza Mayor y la Universidad. Cena y alojamiento en el Parador Nacional.

Dia 10 – SALAMANCA - BAYONA O CAMBADOS.
Desayuno. Salida vía Zamora y Puebla de Sanabria hacia Galicia, donde llegamos a las rías Bajas. Cena y alojamiento en el Parador Nacional de Bayona o Cambados.

Dia 11– BAYONA O CAMBADOS - SANTIAGO DE COMPOSTELA.
Desayuno. Salida hacia la isla de La Toja, con su famoso Balneario. Continuación a Santiago de Compostela. Por la tarde, visita de la ciudad, la Basilica, la Universidad. Cena y alojamiento en el famoso Parador Nacional de los Reyes Católicos.

Dia 12– SANTIAGO DE COMPOSTELA - LEON
Desayuno. Mañana libre en la ciudad, por la tarde, salida a León. Cena y alojamiento en el bello Parador Nacional de San Marcos.

Dia 13– LEON - MADRID
Desayuno. Tiempo libre para recorrer la ciudad y su bella catedral. Salida a Tordesillas y Madrid. Llegada. Alojamiento en el hotel.

Dia 14– MADRID
Desayuno. Por la mañana, visita de la ciudad, recorrido por las calles principales, visitando la famosa pinacoteca de El Prado, así como el Palacio Real. Tarde libre. Alojamiento en el hotel.

Dia 15– MADRID
Desayuno. Tiempo libre- Regreso a América.

SALIDAS: Domingos
Mayo 21; Junio 25; Julio 2, 9, 23; Agosto 6, 20; Sep 3, 17; Octubre 1, 15

PRECIO POR PERSONA	
NEW YORK	$2083
MIAMI	2140
Tierra solo	1461
Sencillo adic.	450
Aumento terrestre 7/1-8/20	85

NUESTROS HOTELES	
MADRID	El Coloso 1*
CORDOBA	P. N. de la Arruzafa 1*
GRANADA	Alhambra Palace 1*
COSTA DEL SOL	Meliá Costa del Sol 1*
SEVILLA	Meliá Sevilla 1*
MERIDA	P. N. Vía de la Plata 1*
SALAMANCA	P. N. de Salamanca 1*
BAYONA	P. N. Conde de Gondomar 1*
LA TOJA	Gran hotel Lujo
CAMBADOS	P. N. el Albariño TS
SANTIAGO DE COMPOSTELA	Los Reyes Católicos Lujo/ Hotel Compostela/ Peregrino 1*
LEON	P. N. San Marcos Lujo/ Hotel Conde Luna 1*

NOTA: Las salidas de julio 23 y agosto 6 se alojarán en el gran Hotel de La Toja en lugar del Parador de Bayona.
Las salidas de junio 25, julio 9, septiembre 3 y 17 se alojarán en el Hotel Compostela en lugar del Parador de Santiago.
Las salidas julio 9, agosto 20 y septiembre 3 se alojarán en el Parador de Cambados, en lugar de Bayona.
La salida de octubre 1 se alojará en Hotel Conde Luna de León en lugar del Parador Nacional.

Nombre ______________________ Fecha ______________

Después de leer

W13-9 Imagínese que usted fue a España con el paquete anterior que ofrece la agencia de viajes en **Vamos a leer.** Seleccione una ciudad y escríbale una tarjeta postal a un(a) amigo(a) desde esa ciudad. Mencione los lugares que visitó, las actividades que hizo, etcétera.

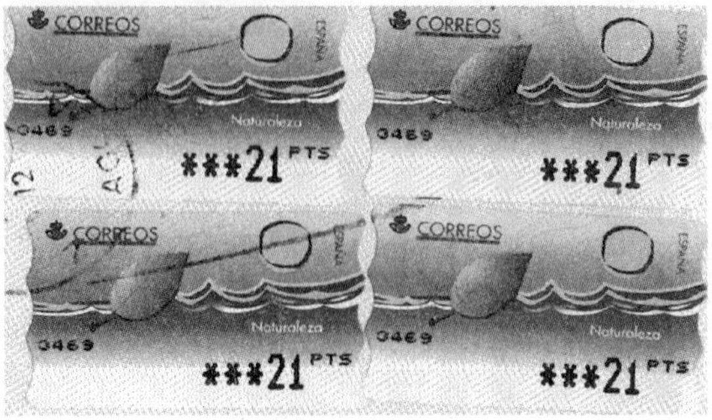

Nombre ______________________ Fecha __________

¡A escribir!

Antes de escribir

W13-10 Lea los anuncios de varios hoteles y balnearios *(resorts)* en la página siguiente y conteste las preguntas a continuación.

1. ¿En qué lugar se puede hacer excursiones a caballo?
____
2. ¿Cuál de los hoteles está al lado del mar?
____
3. ¿Qué hotel tiene las habitaciones a mejor precio?
____
4. ¿Dónde se puede cocinar dentro de la habitación?
____
5. ¿En cuál de estos hoteles le gustaría quedarse a Ud.? ¿Por qué?
____

Phrases: planning a vacation
Vocabulary: traveling
Grammar: verbs; subjunctive with conjunctions; subjunctive with **ojalá;** subjunctive with **que**

Hotel Real Miramar

le invita a descansar al lado del mar
y a disfrutar las brisas caribeñas

- 203 habitaciones de lujo
- Conserje las veinticuatro horas
- Servicio de lavandería y tintorería
- Restaurante/Bar
- Minidiscoteca

¡Deje los quehaceres de la vida cotidiana y disfrute de unas vacaciones de primera!

Habitaciones de U$S 87 a U$S 130

Llame para hacer su reservación hoy al 52-94-89 o al 52-94-92

Descanse y disfrute...

Nuestra hacienda cuenta con cinco habitaciones en la casa grande y cuatro cabañas privadas, cada uno con dos dormitorios y cocina propia.

Descanse en los jardines, al lado de la pileta, o en la biblioteca.

Si es aventurero, explore el monte en excursiones a caballo. Nuestros guías son oriundos del lugar y conocen los sitios más bonitos de la región.

...como sólo lo puede hacer en la Hacienda El Monte

Reserve hoy su habitación. Llame al 304-94-68.

¡Precio especial: cabaña $99.00 la noche!

ALBERGUE DE LA PLAZA

¡QUÉDESE CON NOSTROS Y NO SE PIERDA NADA!

Ubicado en el centro de la ciudad, nuestro albergue ofrece lo mejor en precio y localidad. A meros pasos de los más movidos restaurantes, bares, discotecas y centros comerciales de la ciudad, también estamos muy cerca de museos y otras diversiones turísticas.

Servicios

- teléfono y TV en la habitación
- fax y fotocopiadora en el lobby
- piscina y sauna
- guardería infantil
- alquiler de bicicletas y vespas

¡Todo por tan sólo 79 dólares la noche!
LLAME AL 37-93-85

Nombre ______________________ Fecha ____________

Vamos a escribir

W13-11 Todos deseamos ir a pasar unas vacaciones maravillosas algún día. Escriba en su diario en forma detallada cómo quiere que sea su viaje ideal. Incluya lo siguiente para describir el viaje:

- a qué país o lugar quiere ir
- cuándo y cómo quiere viajar
- quién quiere que vaya con usted y por qué
- cómo quiere que sea el hotel y dónde quiere que esté
- qué facilidades desea que tenga la habitación de su hotel
- qué es posible que usted haga durante su viaje ideal

Mi diario

Mi viaje ideal

Nombre ______________________________ Fecha ______________

Después de escribir

W13-12 Ahora escriba brevemente una experiencia que usted tuvo durante un viaje. Puede ser una experiencia positiva o negativa. Comparta esta experiencia con un(a) compañero(a) de clase.

____

____

____

____

____

____

____

____

____

____

____

____

W13-13 Lectura. Mire la Guía de Servicios en la próxima página y haga los ejercicios que siguen.

1. Los números que aparecen en la lectura son...
   a. los números de las habitaciones.
   b. los números de las extensiones telefónicas del hotel.
   c. los pisos donde se encuentran los servicios.
2. Mire los servicios que aparecen en el directorio. ¿Qué servicios corresponden a las siguientes actividades?
   a. nadar ____________________
   b. cuidar niños ____________________
   c. lavar la ropa ____________________
   d. jugar juegos electrónicos ____________________
   e. dejar el dinero y las joyas con el hotel ____________________
3. ¿A qué número llama usted para los siguientes servicios?
   ________ a. para pedir toallas extras
   ________ b. si usted está enfermo(a)
   ________ c. si quiere hacer una reservación en el restaurante
4. ¿Qué servicios requieren reservaciones?

   ____

Nombre ______________________ Fecha ____________

Guía de Servicios

9	INFORMACION	**Para estos servicios marque Ext. 9**
9	DE CUARTO A CUARTO	**Oficina de Reservaciones** LOCALIZADA JUNTO A RECEPCION HORARIO DE 9:00 am. A 16:00 pm.
0	LLAMADAS LOCALES	**Servicio de Botones** ANEXO A RECEPCION
9	LARGA DISTANCIA	**Cajas de Seguridad** SERVICIO LAS 24 HORAS
9	DESPERTADOR	**Servicio de Niñeras** COMUNICARSE CON EL AMA DE LLAVE CON ANTICIPACION DE 5 HORAS
6	RECEPCION	**Natación** DOS ALBERCAS DE 9:00 am A 22:00 p.m. NO SE PERMITE QUE NIÑOS MENORES DE 12 AÑOS, UTILICEN LAS ALBERCAS SOLOS.
5	LOBBY ACUEDUCTO	**Lavandería y Tintorería** RECIBO 10:00 am. ENTREGA 21:30 p.m. SERVICIO DE LUNES A SABADO
1	AMA DE LLAVES	**Sala de juegos** SERVICIO DE 9:00 am. A 24:00 p.m. LOCALIZADA EN LA SECCION ACUEDUCTO BOLICHE, PING-PONG, DOMINO, JUEGOS ELECTRONICOS, CARTAS.
2	SERVICIO DE CUARTOS	**Servicio Médico** EL HOTEL PROPORCIONA EL SERVICIO LAS 24 HORAS, CON EL GERENTE DE TURNO
4	SERVI-BAR	**Correo** ENTREGA DE CORRESPONDENCIA EN LA RECEPCION DEL HOTEL.
8	RESTAURANT "LA FONDA"	**Agencia de Viajes** VIAJES H.R., S.A. DE 9:00 am. A 17 pm. RENTA DE AUTOMOVILES TRANSPORTACION AL AEROPUERTO DE MEXICO RESERVACIONES DE BOLETO DE AVION
3	BAR "LA TABERNA"	**Objetos Perdidos** EL HOTEL NO SE HACE RESPONSABLE POR DINERO, JOYAS U OBJETOS DE VALOR EXTRAVIADOS EN EL HOTEL. SIN EMBARGO PUEDE COMUNICARSE A RELACIONES PUBLICAS
5	LOBBY BAR "LA ESTANCIA"	**Oficina de Ventas** DE LUNES A SABADO HORARIO DE 9:30 am. A 18:00 p.m.
		Servicio de Convenciones COPIADORAS Y ENMICADOS, ACETATOS PIZARRONES, ETC.

Nombre ______________________ Fecha ______________

Actividades y ejercicios orales

En contexto

CD2-31 **W13-14** **¡Te esperamos en Galicia!** Escuche la siguiente conversación. Decida si las siguientes oraciones son verdaderas **(V)**, falsas **(F)** o si no hay suficiente información **(N)** para contestar.

1. ______ Ileana va a visitar a sus tíos en Madrid.
2. ______ El tío Manuel mandó información sobre los hostales en Madrid.
3. ______ Ileana quiere quedarse en Madrid más de una semana.
4. ______ Ileana desea visitar a los primos por más de dos semanas.
5. ______ Ileana quiere celebrar las fiestas de Santiago de Compostela con los tíos y los primos.

Vocabulario esencial

CD2-32 **W13-15** **¡Bienvenidos al Hostal Azul!** Escuche la siguiente conversación por teléfono entre Ileana Gamboa, que está haciendo reservaciones, y el recepcionista del Hostal Azul. Escriba la información que el recepcionista necesita tener en el formulario del hotel.

Reservación

Nombre ______________________

Dirección ______________________

Ciudad ______________________

País ______________________

Día de llegada ______________________

Preferencia: Sencilla ______

Doble ______

Triple ______

Nombre ______________________ Fecha ______________

CD2-33 **W13-16 Situaciones en el Hostal Azul.** Escuche las cinco conversaciones sobre lo que pasa en el Hostal Azul y escriba el número debajo del dibujo correspondiente abajo y en la próxima página. No se van a usar todos los dibujos.

a. __________

b. __________

c. __________

d. __________

Nombre ______________________ Fecha ______________

CD2-34 **W13-17 La vida en España.** Usted va a escuchar cinco oraciones sobre la vida en España. Reaccione a cada oración según su opinión. Comience su respuesta con **Dudo que... , No dudo que... , Creo que...** o **No estoy seguro(a) que...**.

Ejemplo: En España todos los hoteles son muy caros.
Dudo que todos los hoteles sean muy caros.

1. ____
____
2. ____
____
3. ____
____
4. ____
____
5. ____
____

Nombre ______________________ Fecha ______________

LECCIÓN 14 ¡LO SIENTO, PERO NO ME SIENTO BIEN!

Cuaderno de ejercicios

VOCABULARIO ESENCIAL

W14-1 Enfermedades y sus remedios. Complete las siguientes oraciones sobre enfermedades con la palabra correcta de la lista.

dolor de cabeza
insomnio
náuseas
catarro
dolor de muela
una receta médica

1. Cuando Alicia tiene ______________________, tiene que ir al dentista.
2. Si Alicia y Mariana tienen ______________________, necesitan tomar pastillas para la tos *(cough drops)*.
3. Alicia tiene ______________________; por eso va a tomar aspirina.
4. El año pasado, Mariana tuvo dolor de oído y fiebre, por eso el médico le dio ______________________ para antibióticos.
5. Cuando Mariana tiene ______________________, ella toma Pepto-Bismol.
6. Cuando una persona no puede dormir tiene ______________________.

W14-2 Había muchos pacientes en la clínica. Cuando Alicia y Mariana fueron a la clínica, vieron a muchos pacientes allí con todo tipo de problemas médicos. Mire los dibujos en la próxima página y describa los problemas de cada paciente, según el número indicado.

Ejemplo: ¿Qué tiene la paciente número uno?
La mujer está embarazada y tiene tos.

Nombre ______________________ Fecha ______________

1. ¿Qué tiene el paciente número dos?

____

____

2. ¿Qué tiene la paciente número tres?

____

____

3. ¿Qué tiene el paciente número cuatro?

____

____

4. ¿Qué tiene la paciente número cinco?

____

____

W14-3 ¿Qué hace usted cuando... ? Escriba una respuesta para cada pregunta sobre problemas médicos.

Ejemplo: ¿Qué hace usted cuando le duele la cabeza?
Tomo aspirina y me acuesto.

1. ¿Qué hace usted cuando tiene gripe y fiebre alta?

____

2. ¿Qué recomienda usted para el dolor de estómago cuando uno come mucho?

____

3. ¿Qué hace usted cuando tiene mucha tos y fiebre?

____

4. ¿Qué hace usted cuando le duelen las piernas porque hizo mucho ejercicio?

____

GRAMÁTICA ESENCIAL

W14-4 ¡Qué lástima! Alicia y Mariana están expresando cómo se sintieron durante sus vacaciones. Escriba oraciones utilizando las siguientes palabras y expresiones. Incluya la forma correcta del verbo en el pasado del subjuntivo.

Ejemplo: fue una lástima que / pasarse / las tres semanas tan pronto
Fue una lástima que se pasaran las tres semanas tan pronto.

1. era imposible que nosotros / visitar / todo Los Ángeles y Arizona en dos semanas

   ____

   ____

2. yo preferiría que la próxima vez / nosotros / estar / allí más de un mes

   ____

   ____

3. fue una lástima que no nosotros / poder / viajar a Nevada también

   ____

   ____

4. ¡qué malo que me / enfermar / del estómago!

   ____

   ____

W14-5 ¿Qué haría usted en estas situaciones? Primero, ponga los verbos entre paréntesis en el condicional para completar las oraciones. Después, decida cuál sería la mejor opción y ponga la letra en el espacio en blanco.

1. __________ Si usted estuviera estudiando en una universidad española y de repente tuviera náuseas, ¿qué haría?

   a. __________ (Beber) leche y __________ (esperar) hasta que me sintiera mejor.

   b. __________ (Tomar) dos aspirinas y __________ (guardar) cama por dos días.

   c. __________ (Ir) a una clínica para que un médico me examinara.

2. __________ Si usted acabara de llegar a un hotel y descubriera que la recepcionista no tiene su reservación y ya no hay un cuarto vacante, ¿qué haría?

   a. Le __________ (pedir) que me permitiera usar el teléfono para llamar a otro hotel.

   b. __________ (Volver) al aeropuerto para comprar un billete y volver a casa.

   c. __________ (Hablar) con el gerente del hotel y le __________ (explicar) el problema.

3. ______________ Si usted fuera doctor(a) y un día un paciente lo visitara porque sufre de un dolor de oído horrible, ¿qué haría?

   a. Le ______________ (dar) dos aspirinas y le ______________ (decir) que me llamara al día siguiente.

   b. Le ______________ (decir) a mi enfermera que le pusiera una inyección.

   c. Le ______________ (examinar) el oído y le ______________ (escribir) una receta médica.

4. Si usted estuviera viajando en el extranjero y perdiera sus cheques de viajero, ¿qué haría?

   a. ______________ (Ir) al banco con la lista de los números de mis cheques.

   b. ______________ (Llamar) a mis padres y les ______________ (pedir) más dinero.

   c. ______________ (Ir) a hablar con la policía y ______________ (llenar) un formulario en caso de que los encontraran.

W14-6 Descansaría mucho... Conteste las siguientes preguntas sobre lo que haría usted si tuviera gripe.

Ejemplo: Si usted tuviera gripe...
¿iría a una clínica médica o a un hospital?
Si yo tuviera gripe, iría a una clínica médica.

Si usted tuviera gripe...

1. ¿tendría temperatura o le dolería la cabeza?

   ____

2. ¿tomaría pastillas o preferiría una inyección?

   ____

3. ¿descansaría un poco o volvería a trabajar inmediatamente?

   ____

4. ¿le pagaría al médico al contado o usaría su tarjeta de crédito?

   ____

CULTURA

W14-7 Por el mundo hispano. Conteste estas preguntas según la información cultural de la **Lección 14.**

1. En Latinoamérica, los médicos y especialistas cobran (mucho / poco) en comparación con los Estados Unidos y Canadá.
2. En muchas partes del mundo hispano, los farmacéuticos (pueden / no pueden) dar consejos y vender medicinas sin receta médica.
3. Si estás en el extranjero, necesitas beber agua (de botella / del grifo) para evitar "el turista".
4. Antes de comer, es recomendable ______________ las manos. También es mejor ______________ y ______________ las frutas y vegetales.

Nombre ______________________ Fecha ______________

W14-8 Lectura. Mire el anuncio de aspirinas y conteste las preguntas.

1. ¿Cuántas aspirinas se consumen en el mundo cada día?

   ____

2. ¿Cuántos millones de dólares se gastan en los Estados Unidos en aspirinas?

   ____

3. ¿Cuántas aspirinas toman los españoles como promedio al año?

   ____

4. ¿Quiénes llevaron aspirinas a la Luna?

   ____

5. ¿Desde hace cuántos años se usa la aspirina?

   ____

La aspirina llegó a la Luna

La aspirina se popularizó rápidamente. A principios del siglo XX, con las epidemias de gripe, se utiliza ya masivamente en Europa y en los Estados Unidos. En este país, devastado por una gripe en la década de los cincuenta, la fábrica de aspirina estuvo días fabricando comprimidos *(pills)* ininterrupidamente día y noche debido a la gran demanda.

Después de casi cien años la aspirina incluso ha viajado al espacio: los astronautas Armstrong, Aldrin y Collins, los primeros seres humanos que pisaron la Luna, llevaban en el botiquín del Apolo XI, entre otras cosas, varias aspirinas.

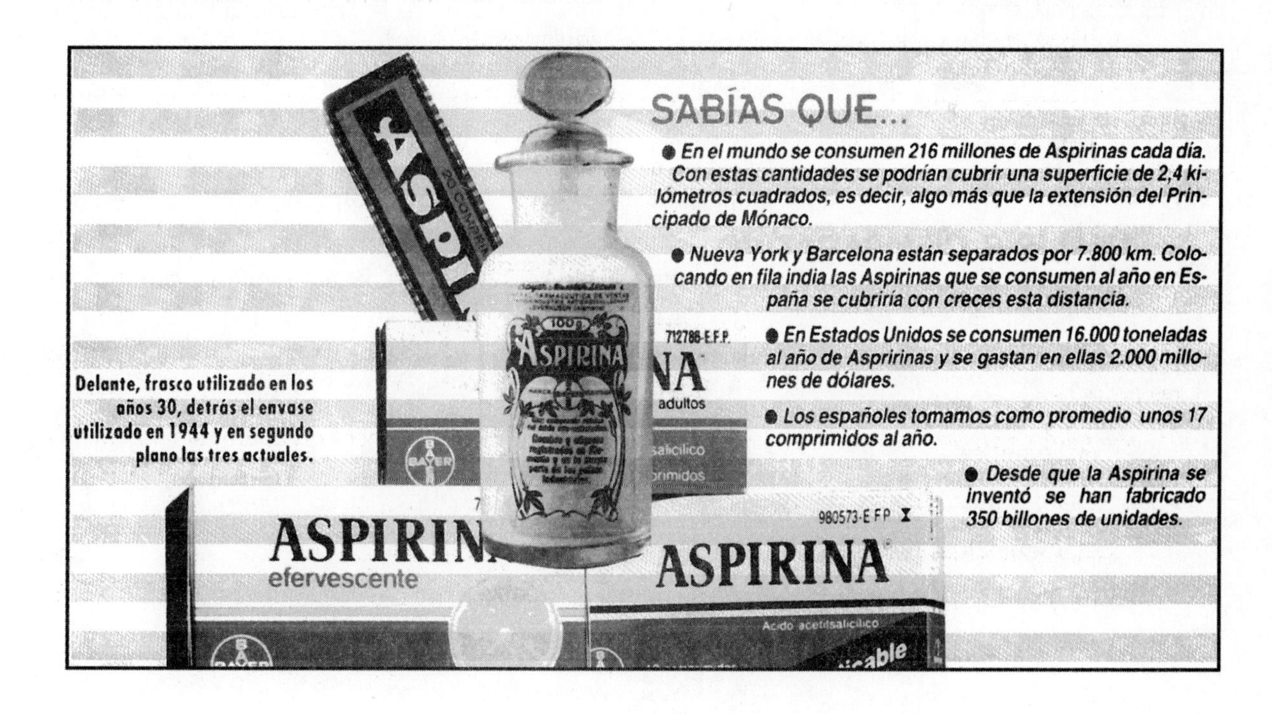

Delante, frasco utilizado en los años 30, detrás el envase utilizado en 1944 y en segundo plano las tres actuales.

Nombre ______________________________ Fecha ______________

¡A leer!: Médico de familia

Antes de leer

W14-9 En muchas revistas se puede encontrar secciones escritas por médicos o especialistas dedicadas a responder a las preguntas médicas de los lectores *(readers)*. ¿Qué tipo de información piensa usted que se puede encontrar en una sección médica?

____

____

____

W14-10 Muchos factores determinan la presión sanguínea *(blood pressure)* de una persona. Algunos son más fáciles de controlar que otros. ¿Qué tipo de factores cree usted que se afectan la presión?

_______ genéticos

_______ climáticos

_______ dietéticos

_______ relacionados con la vida del individuo

_______ hormonales

_______ emocionales

_______ educacionales

W14-11 Hoy en día se puede encontrar a muchas personas que sufren de senilidad. ¿Qué factores cree usted que puedan ser la causa de la pérdida de la memoria?

_______ la enfermedad de Alzheimer

_______ los problemas de tiroides *(thyroid gland)*

_______ la obesidad

_______ las drogas

_______ la falta de ejercicio

_______ los problemas del corazón

_______ las depresiones

_______ el alcohol

_______ la nutrición deficiente

_______ las infecciones

Vamos a leer

W14-12 Mire los factores que usted seleccionó en la parte anterior como factores que tienen influencia en la presión sanguínea.

1. Corrija su lista, según los que menciona el Médico de Familia de la página siguiente con un bolígrafo *(pen)* de color diferente.
2. ¿Qué le aconseja el médico que haga para bajar *(to lower)* la presión?

_______ bajar de peso

_______ comer sal

_______ no fumar

_______ tomar alcohol con moderación

_______ mantenerse en forma, haciendo ejercicios

P **Tengo 43 años de edad y en mi último examen clínico una enfermera me comentó que tenía la presión un poco alta. Pero solo me aconsejó que eliminara la sal en las comidas. ¿Qué debo hacer para bajar mi presión alta?**

(Gonzalo Torres)

R La presión sanguínea es determinada por factores genéticos, hormonales, emocionales, y relacionados con el tipo de vida del paciente. Los médicos no tienen control sobre todos estos factores, aunque sí pueden ser influenciados. A continuación le damos unos consejos que le ayudarán a bajar su presión sanguínea y a mantenerla normal:

- Elimine el exceso de peso. Guíese por las tablas de talla y peso para que sepa cuál es su peso ideal. Disminuya el consumo de grasas y aumente el de frutas y vegetales.
- Tome alcohol con moderación (no más de dos tragos diarios).
- ¡No fume!
- Haga ejercicios. Si no está "en forma", pregunte al médico qué tipo de ejercicios y qué intensidad es saludable para usted.
- Y, como ya le ha dicho su enfermera, elimine sal en su dieta; restrinja los alimentos preparados con sal (utilice muy poca o ninguna sal en la cocina o en la mesa).

P **Mi madre está perdiendo la memoria y yo estoy muy preocupada por la posibilidad de que tenga la *enfermedad de Alzheimer.* Se sabe muy poco sobre esta enfermedad, pero... ¿qué puedo hacer para ayudarla?**

(Rosario Peñalver)

R Primero que todo, usted no debe presumir que su madre tiene la *enfermedad de Alzheimer*, ni tampoco que la senilidad es una parte inevitable del paso de los años o envejecimiento. Tenga en cuenta que sólo un 10% de las personas mayores de 65 años padecen de senilidad, y que la *enfermedad de Alzheimer* es solamente una de las muchas posibles causas de esta declinación. La pérdida de la memoria, rasgo principal de la senilidad, es a menudo el resultado de condiciones que son reversibles. Es decir, que esta pérdida puede ser efectivamente tratada.

Le sugerimos que lleve a su madre a un buen especialista. La pérdida de la memoria puede ser causada por muchos factores, los cuales incluyen: problemas del corazón, infecciones, mal funcionamiento de la tiroides, nutrición deficiente y depresiones. A esta lista se agrega el consumo de alcohol y ciertos medicamentos utilizados para combatir el insomnio, calmar los nervios, reducir la acidez estomacal o disminuir los temblores. Todas estas sustancias pueden afectar la memoria, especialmente en las personas de edad avanzada.

Si después de un examen general no se encuentran causas físicas o sicológicas de esta pérdida de la memoria, entonces su madre debe ser vista por un neurólogo. Es conveniente que tome algunas notas sobre el patrón de la pérdida de memoria en su madre antes de llevarla al especialista. Tenga en cuenta, al hacerlo, si el cambio ha sido drástico o es la continuación de viejos problemas; si está deprimida o siente soledad; si le faltan estímulos intelectuales; etc. Trate de dar la mayor información posible al médico; su participación será de gran valor en el desarrollo de un plan de tratamiento. ¡Son muchas las cosas que pueden hacerse para mejorar la memoria de una persona!

W14-13 ¿Qué le preocupa a la persona que escribió la segunda carta?

____

____

W14-14 Mire los factores que usted seleccionó en la parte anterior como los que pueden causar la pérdida de memoria.

1. Corrija su lista, según los que menciona el Médico de Familia con un bolígrafo de color distinto.
2. Si después de un examen general no se encuentra causa para la pérdida de memoria, ¿a quién debe ver la paciente?

   ____

Después de leer

W14-15 Escriba una carta breve al Médico de Familia. Invente una persona ficticia y una enfermedad. Incluya su edad y cualquier otra información médica que necesite saber el médico.

Nombre ______________________ Fecha ____________

W14-16 Responda a la carta como si usted fuera el Médico de Familia. Respóndale al (a la) paciente con las recomendaciones apropiadas.

Nombre ______________________________ Fecha ______________

¡A escribir!

Antes de escribir

W14-17 Complete las siguientes oraciones con información sobre su juventud.

En mi familia

1. Yo no quería que ______________________________.
2. Me gustaba que ______________________________.
3. Era importante que ______________________________.

En la escuela

4. Los profesores preferían que ______________________________.
5. Mis amigos no creían que ______________________________.
6. Yo no estaba seguro(a) de que ______________________________.

Mis pasatiempos y deportes

7. Mis padres me prohibían que ______________________________.
8. Para mí era importante que ______________________________.
9. Mis amigos querían que yo ______________________________.

Phrases: describing the past; talking about habitual actions; talking about past events
Vocabulary: leisure; sports; studies
Grammar: verbs: preterite & imperfect, subjunctive agreement

Vamos a escribir

W14-18 En la próxima página, escriba en su diario sobre las emociones, los sentimientos y las opiniones que usted tenía cuando era joven. Incluya la información anterior y agregue otra información apropiada.

Nombre ______________________ Fecha ______________

Mi diario

Nombre ______________________________ Fecha ______________

Después de escribir

W14-19 En su diario, busque todas las frases que requieren el subjuntivo y haga un círculo alrededor de ellas. Escríbalas en las lineas que aparecen a continuación. Después, haga una lista con todos los verbos que siguen estas frases. ¿Usó usted el pasado del subjuntivo? ¿Escribió correctamente estos verbos? Corríjalos si es necesario.

Las expresiones y frases que requieren el subjuntivo	La forma del pasado del subjuntivo correspondiente
Ejemplo: *Ojalá que no me duela el estómago.*	*Ojalá que no me doliera el estómago.*
______________________________	______________________________
______________________________	______________________________
______________________________	______________________________
______________________________	______________________________
______________________________	______________________________
______________________________	______________________________
______________________________	______________________________
______________________________	______________________________
______________________________	______________________________
______________________________	______________________________
______________________________	______________________________
______________________________	______________________________
______________________________	______________________________

Nombre ______________________ Fecha ______________

Actividades y ejercicios orales

En contexto

CD2-35 **W14-20** **¡Lo siento, pero no me siento bien!** Escuche la siguiente conversación. Decida si las siguientes oraciones son verdaderas **(V)**, falsas **(F)** o si no hay suficiente información **(N)** para contestar.

1. ________ Mariana siempre come comida del Caribe.
2. ________ A Alicia no le gusta la comida caribeña.
3. ________ A Alicia le duele el estómago desde hace varios días.
4. ________ Mariana quiere llevar a Alicia a su médico.
5. ________ El médico trabaja cerca de la casa de Mariana.

Vocabulario esencial

CD2-36 **W14-21** **La médica me dijo que me cuidara.** Alicia vio a la médica y luego Mariana le hizo varias preguntas. Escuche la siguiente conversación y responda a las siguientes preguntas.

1. ¿Por qué fue Alicia a ver a la médica?
   ____
2. ¿Qué le recomendó la médica para el dolor de estómago?
   ____
3. ¿Qué le recomendó la médica que hiciera para el dolor de espalda?
   ____

CD2-37 **W14-22** **La Clínica Buena Vista.** La secretaria de la Clínica Buena Vista recibe varias llamadas telefónicas. Escúchelas y luego escriba a continuación lo que dicen las pacientes.

Nombre ______________________________ Fecha ______________

CD2-38 **W14-23 Doctor, el (la) paciente dijo que...** Escuche otra vez las conversaciones telefónicas de la Clínica Buena Vista y complete las siguientes frases.

La llamada de la señora García

1. _______ La señora García toma...
   a. aspirinas para el dolor de cabeza.
   b. pastillas para la infección en los oídos.
   c. medicina para el dolor de estómago.

2. _______ La secretaria le dijo a la señora Gracía que...
   a. esperara la llamada del doctor Ramírez.
   b. fuera a la clínica para una cita.
   c. hiciera una cita con el médico.

La llamada del señor Perdomo

3. _______ El señor Perdomo quería que...
   a. la secretaria le diera la medicina.
   b. el doctor Anaya lo llamara por teléfono.
   c. la secretaria le hiciera una cita para ver al doctor.

4. _______ El señor Perdomo dijo que tenía...
   a. dolor de estómago, náuseas y fiebre.
   b. dolor de cabeza y fiebre.
   c. dolor de espalda.

La llamada de la señora Álvarez

5. _______ La señora Álvarez quiere ver al médico para que...
   a. le dé unas medicinas para la gripe.
   b. vea a su niño.
   c. la examine a ella.

6. _______ Al hijo de la señora Álvarez le duele...
   a. el estómago.
   b. la garganta.
   c. los oídos.

Nombre ______________________ Fecha ____________

LECCIÓN 15 ¿QUÉ PODRÍAMOS HACER NOSOTROS POR NUESTRO MEDIO AMBIENTE?

Cuaderno de ejercicios

VOCABULARIO ESENCIAL

W15-1 Reacciones. Escriba sobre algunos de los problemas del mundo y de los Estados Unidos. También diga cómo le afectan a usted personalmente. Use las frases y el vocabulario de las siguientes listas.

Siento que...	la delincuencia
Es malo que...	la guerra
Me molesta que...	la pobreza
Es una lástima que...	el terrorismo
Me preocupa que...	la discriminación
Es importante que...	la contaminación del medio ambiente

1. ______________________________

2. ______________________________

3. ______________________________

4. ______________________________

5. ______________________________

6. ______________________________

Nombre ______________________ Fecha __________

W15-2 Observaciones personales. Indique dónde vio o ve usted cada uno de los siguientes problemas. Utilice los lugares de la lista u otros lugares que usted conozca.

Ejemplo: ver / pobreza
Vi la pobreza en Chicago, en Calcutta y en la Ciudad de México. Veo pobreza en mi ciudad todos los días.

África	la China	la India
Arabia Saudita	Colombia	Irlanda
Bosnia	Egipto	el Japón
el Brasil	los Estados Unidos	(otro país o lugar)

1. ver / en la televisión / haber guerra

____
____
____

2. ver / haber / deshechos tóxicos

____
____
____

3. ver / discriminación racial

____
____
____

4. observar / destrucción de la naturaleza

____
____
____

5. ver / haber escasez ***(scarcity)*** de recursos naturales

____
____
____

6. ver / contaminación del medio ambiente

____
____
____

Nombre ______________________________ Fecha ______________

Gramática esencial

W15-3 **¿Qué haría usted?** Complete las siguientes oraciones con información sobre lo que usted haría si estuviera en las siguientes situaciones.

Ejemplo: Si yo fuera presidente de los Estados Unidos,
les daría suficientes fondos a las grandes ciudades para que hubiera más medios de transporte público.

1. Si yo viviera en un lugar que tuviera mucha contaminación del aire,
____
______________________________.
2. Si yo fuera multimillonario(a),
____
______________________________.
3. Si yo fuera a vivir a otro planeta y sólo pudiera llevar cinco cosas,
____
______________________________.
4. Si yo fuera científico(a),
____
______________________________.
5. Si yo tuviera la oportunidad de hacer contribuciones humanitarias en este momento,
____
______________________________.

W15-4 **Situaciones.** Lea cada situación. Luego complete las oraciones lógicamente, usando los verbos de las listas.

1. volver / tener / regresar

   Ileana se quedaría en Santiago de Compostela si ella no...

   ______________ que terminar sus estudios.

   ______________ a la universidad.

   ______________ a Costa Rica para trabajar.

2. tener / poder / conocer / encontrar

   Alicia y David harían un viaje a Venezuela si ellos...

   ______________ ahorrar más dinero.

   ______________ un trabajo en Caracas.

   ______________ un trabajo en Caracas.

   ______________ a muchas personas allí.

Nombre ______________________ Fecha ____________

W15-5 Fin de vacaciones. Ileana y Alicia regresaron a Madison, Wisconsin, para terminar sus estudios y ahora están conversando sobre sus experiencias en México y en España. Complete las siguientes oraciones con la forma correcta del pasado del subjuntivo de los verbos de la lista. Se puede usar un verbo más de una vez.

ir	traer
pasar	ver
poder	viajar
tener	

Ejemplo: Alicia: ¡Qué lástima que David y yo no ***fuéramos*** a Venezuela!

Ileana: Sí, pero me alegré que ustedes ____________ pasar tres semanas juntos en Chile.

Alicia: Sí, es verdad, estuvimos en Santiago y lo pasamos muy bien. Y a ti, Ileana, ¿no te molestó que no ____________ viajar a Barcelona o Sevilla?

Ileana: No, fue bueno que no ____________ a otros lugares porque así tuve más tiempo con mis primos y mis tíos. Además, mi mamá quería que yo ____________ unas vacaciones tranquilas.

Alicia: De acuerdo, pero mi mamá quería que yo ____________ muchos lugares por si acaso no puedo regresar.

Ileana: Sí, y fue importante que yo te ____________ esta revista para que ____________ los lugares donde puedes trabajar en Latinoamérica con niños.

Alicia: Sí, Ileana, eres una amiga. ¡Pura vida!, como dicen en tu país.

W15-6 Especulaciones. ¿Cómo será la vida de los amigos que conocimos en este libro? Especule sobre la vida de ellos.

Ejemplo: Alicia Benson regresa a los Estados Unidos a terminar sus estudios.
Deseo que ***ella tenga la oportunidad de volver a Latinoamérica.***
Ojalá que ***ella y David puedan ir algún día a Venezuela.***

1. Luis Chávez no sabe qué quiere hacer cuando termine sus estudios.

   Le aconsejo que ____.

   ____

   Espero que ____.

   ____

2. David Kerr quiere regresar a Chile para trabajar en el viñedo de los señores Torreón.

   Es bueno que ____.

   ____

   Es posible que ____.

   ____

3. El señor Gildo Navarro y su hija María Alexandra piensan comprar un mercado más grande.

   Estoy seguro(a) que ________________________________.

   ____

   Les aconsejo que ________________________________.

   ____

4. Enrique y Gloria León van a invertir mucho dinero en la exportación de café colombiano a los Estados Unidos.

   Es probable que ________________________________.

   ____

   Me alegro de que ________________________________.

   ____

5. Ileana Gamboa quiere regresar a España para trabajar y vivir.

   Es importante que ________________________________.

   ____

   Le recomiendo que ________________________________.

   ____

CULTURA

W15-7 Por el mundo hispano. Conteste las siguientes preguntas sobre las lecturas culturales de la **Lección 15.**

1. ¿Puede explicar lo que es "La educación sin fronteras"?

   ____

2. ¿Le gustaría a usted participar en este tipo de organización algún día? ¿Por qué sí o por qué no?

   ____

   ____

3. ¿Puede usted describir cómo el ruido puede contaminar el ambiente?

   ____

4. ¿Cuáles son algunos efectos que tiene la contaminación por el ruido?

   ____

   ____

Nombre ______________________ Fecha ______________

¡A leer!: Veraneantes solidarios

Antes de leer

W15-8 El trabajo de verano. Conteste las preguntas antes de leer el artículo.

1. ¿Qué tipo de trabajo puede hacer usted en sus vacaciones de verano?

____

____

2. ¿Le gustaría viajar a un país en vía de desarrollo ***(developing country)*** y ayudar a estas personas?

____

____

3. Mire las dos fotos en el artículo de la página siguiente y lea la descripción de las fotos. ¿Qué tipo de trabajo hacen muchos jóvenes españoles? ¿Le gustaría hacer este tipo de trabajo?

____

____

Vamos a leer

W15-9 Mire el artículo en la próxima página mientras hace lo siguiente.

1. Mire el título y las fotos de la lectura de la página siguiente. ¿Quiénes están en las fotos?

____

____

2. ¿Qué trabajo se puede hacer durante las vacaciones de verano?

____

____

3. ¿Qué se requiere para inscribirse en estos programas?

____

____

____

4. Describa los diferentes trabajos que usted podría hacer en estos proyectos.

____

____

____

____

Nombre ______________________ Fecha ______________

¿QUIÉNES SON?

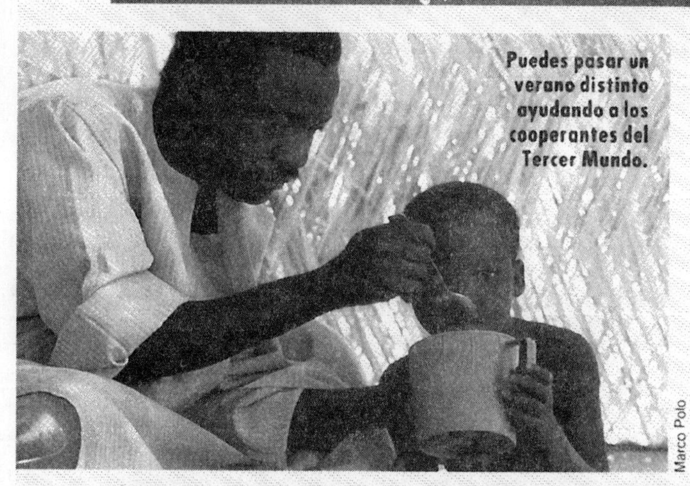

Puedes pasar un verano distinto ayudando a los cooperantes del Tercer Mundo.

Cientos de jóvenes españoles pasan sus vacaciones en algún lugar del Tercer Mundo, para echar una mano allí donde los necesitan y, de paso, conocer una realidad muy distinta a la de nuestro país.

Veraneantes solidarios

Unas vacaciones imborrables

Cada año, durante estos meses de verano, varias organizaciones no gubernamentales (ONG) organizan campos de trabajo y viajes solidarios a diferentes proyectos que ellas mismas u otras organizaciones ya tienen en marcha. Cientos de jóvenes de todo el país se apuntan a estas originales vacaciones, que no son precisamente baratas, ya que si bien la comida y el alojamiento corren a cargo de la organización, el viaje es por cuenta del cooperante. Generalmente se trata de estancias cortas que no superan el mes. Los jóvenes realizan tareas de apoyo a los cooperantes profesionales responsables del proyecto.

¿Qué se requiere para apuntarse?

Como norma general, ser mayor de 21 años, asistir a unos cursos o de preparación y, sobre todo, tener muchas ganas de participar en proyectos de este tipo. Ya a principios de año las organizaciones empiezan a preparar los viajes, no lo dejes para última hora.

¿Dónde informarme?

Estas son algunas de las organizaciones que suelen admitir cooperantes en verano:

- Servei Civil Internacional (SCI): Carmen, 95 bjos. 2a. 08001 Barcelona. Tel. (93) 441 70 79. Organizan campos de trabajo para voluntarios de cualquier punto de la península, Baleares y Canarias.
- Servicio Tercer Mundo (SETEM): St. Antoni Abat, 49 08001 Barcelona. Tel. (93) 441 53 35. Madrid (91) 549 91 28. Granada (958) 81 89 38. Valencia (96) 361 56 51. Vitoria (945) 12 07 46.
- Solidaridad para el desarrollo y la paz (SODEPAZ): Pez, 9 28004 Madrid. Tel. (91) 522 80 91. Barcelona (93) 268 22 02. Logroño (941) 25 45 07. Navarra (948) 24 12 30. Toledo (925) 35 74 86.

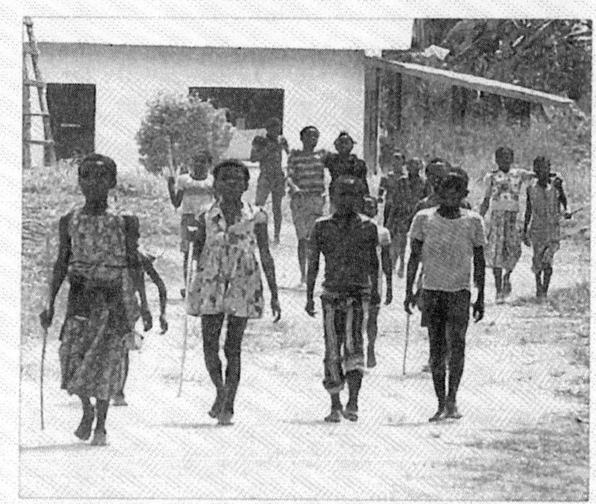
Los campos de trabajo son una experiencia original y solidaria en las vacaciones.

Nombre ______________________________ Fecha ______________

Después de leer

W15-10 Escríbale una carta a la organización de proyectos de verano y explique a qué lugar le gustaría ir a trabajar, por qué y las ideas que usted tiene para ayudar con ese proyecto.

____

____

____

____

____

____

____

____

____

____

____

____

____

____

____

¡A escribir!

Antes de escribir

W15-11 Debemos hacer algo para conservar la Tierra. ¿Cuáles son sus metas ***(goals)*** y planes personales para conservar nuestra Tierra? Llene los espacios en blanco con las cosas que usted quiere hacer.

Para conservar la Tierra y el medio ambiente yo...

1. ____
2. ____
3. ____
4. ____
5. ____

Phrases: animals; means of transportation; plants; working conditions
Grammar: verbs: conditional, subjunctive agreement

Nombre ______________________ Fecha ______________

Vamos a escribir

W15-12 Para usted, ¿cómo sería un mundo perfecto? Escriba un ensayo, usando las siguientes preguntas como guía.

- ¿Qué tipo de clima y ambiente tendría el mundo?
- ¿Cómo serían las ciudades, las escuelas y las casas?
- ¿Qué problemas no existirían más?
- ¿Qué haríamos en el trabajo y para divertirnos?

Nombre ______________________ Fecha ______________

Después de escribir

W15-13 Intercambie su composición con la de un(a) compañero(a) de clase. Lea la nueva composición y compare el mundo de su compañero(a) con su mundo. ¿Tienen estos dos mundos algo en común? ¿Cómo son diferentes? Haga una lista de sus semejanzas ***(similarities)*** y diferencias abajo.

Semejanzas

Diferencias

Nombre ______________________________ Fecha ______________

Actividades y ejercicios orales

En contexto 

CD2-39 **W15-14 El planeta Tierra.** Escuche la siguiente conversación. Decida si las siguientes oraciones son verdaderas **(V)**, falsas **(F)** o si no hay suficiente información **(N)** para contestar.

1. ______ La experiencia de Alicia en Monterrey fue valiosa.
2. ______ Ileana quería quedarse en Santiago de Compostela.
3. ______ Ileana tiene que regresar a Costa Rica para hacer turismo.
4. ______ Alicia quiere trabajar en Latinoamérica toda su vida.
5. ______ Alicia quiere enseñar a los niños latinoamericanos.

Vocabulario esencial 

CD2-40 **W15-15 Las noticias.** Usted va a oír cinco noticias en la radio. Escriba el número de cada noticia debajo del dibujo a que corresponde.

a. ______

b. ______

c. ______

d. ______

e. ______

Nombre ________________________________ Fecha ______________

CD2-41 **W15-16** **¿Qué oyó usted en las noticias?** Escuche otra vez las noticias de la última actividad y conteste las siguientes preguntas.

1. ______ En la noticia número uno el locutor (***announcer***) dijo lo siguiente.
   a. Se inventó un auto nuevo.
   b. Se inventó un motor que usa energía solar.
   c. Se creó un laboratorio nuevo en Alemania.

2. ______ En la noticia número dos se mencionó lo siguiente.
   a. La selva Amazónica se está quemando.
   b. Los árboles en la selva Amazónica están creciendo poco a poco.
   c. El río Amazonas está contaminado.

3. ______ En la noticia número tres se reportó que en la ciudad de Santiago de Chile...
   a. no hay contaminación ambiental.
   b. la ciudad no puede funcionar por cuatro días.
   c. el aire está muy contaminado, en esta época del verano.

4. ______ En la noticia número cuatro se anunció que se puede comprar...
   a. productos biodegradables que ayudan al ambiente.
   b. productos biodegradables que no protegen al ambiente.
   c. productos biodegradables que son muy económicos.

5. ______ La noticia número cinco anunció que en Venezuela...
   a. el agua del Río Orinoco no está contaminada, a pesar de la explotación de recursos renovables.
   b. el agua del Río Orinoco está contaminada debido a la explotación de recursos no renovables.
   c. el agua del Río Orinoco no está contaminada y ayuda a la vida animal de la zona.

CD2-42 **W15-17** **¿Qué cree usted?** Usted va a oír seis oraciones sobre problemas que afectan el mundo y los Estados Unidos. Indique si usted está de acuerdo o no.

Estoy de acuerdo	**No estoy de acuerdo**
1. ______________	______________
2. ______________	______________
3. ______________	______________
4. ______________	______________
5. ______________	______________
6. ______________	______________